HUMAN, WITH A SIDE OF SOUL

H U M A N

With a Side of Soul

One Woman's Soul Quest through
Open-Minded Interviews

GINA DEWINK

Copyright ©2019 by Gina Dewink
All rights reserved. Published in the United States.

isbn 978-0-9989877-5-0 (paperback)
isbn 978-0-9989877-6-7 (ebook)
Library of Congress Control Number: 2019908482

www.ginadewink.com

Book cover design by germancreative
Book layout and formatting by Gessert Books
www.gessertbooks.com

Dedicated to Dad, for instilling a bottomless curiosity in the mysterious and unexplainable.

The mind, once stretched by a new idea, never returns to its original dimensions.

—Ralph Waldo Emerson

Table of

Contents

Introduction

I F THERE WAS a beginner's class—*Soul 101*, let's say—would you sign up to take it? You can pretend it's free. Or online. Or with your best friend. You do you. But are questions about the universe, the afterlife, past lives, near-death experiences, souls or spirits within you?

They were within me. And they led me through a nine-month "semester" of self-driven learning, submerging me in a vast sea of new concepts and foreign ideas. But I knew I wouldn't be able to soak it all in with a purely academic outlook. To best learn, I needed realism and relativity. Creativity. Humor. I needed other quirky, curious humans.

I'm not one for in-depth Biblical studies or debates about God. I am not out to change minds or lives. In fact, this has little-to-nothing to do with religion or belief in God.

What am I here for, then? To learn. And, hopefully, to offer you a basic arsenal of spiritual tools along the way.

Once given the experiences from more than a dozen individuals spanning several walks of life, it will be up to you. What will you accept and what will you reject? What ideas will resonate? What will make your eyes roll?

I am a skeptic with an open mind. A college-educated woman with a great curiosity, but am I an expert in this field? Not at all. Walking into this project, I feel followed by a shadow of ignorance. But the drive to understand is stronger than doubt. My aim is to keep things on the lighter side. To avoid any sort of belittling or condescending. After all, whether a believer, scientist or skeptic, we are all human, and how we communicate means everything. I do not mean to offend. I do not mean to be sacrilegious. I do not mean to be hurtful in any way. I just sincerely want to know... what if everything we need to know is here, and we just need to stop and put the pieces together?

I find it ironic that it takes nine months to cook up a baby, and it took me nine months to create my spiritual base. Along the way, I met amazing humans, tried to communicate with the dead, searched for people I might have been in the past, lost over twenty pounds from my "sack of fat-covered meat" and about a car trunk's worth of mental suitcases. In other words, I changed.

And, perhaps, that's the best—if not only—outcome after a spiritual crash course such as the one I just completed.

Please take your seat. Soul 101 is now in session.

Gina, July 2019

Preparation for

a personal journey

THE WOO-WOO. THAT'S what famed positive speaker and entrepreneur Jack Canfield called it. The strange forces that make things happen when you put the words out there; the law of attraction. Like when you ask a friend at random if she knows of any mindfulness retreats coming up days before she happens to have a second (free) ticket to a Jack Canfield seminar, which is exactly what happened to me. But my woo-woo goes back even farther than that.

In July 2016, I started a new job. After a year as a stay-at-home mom, I had been hired by a small organization with just two other employees (at that time) to direct international communications. I was given the office of a staff member who had just left the company. Being such a small organization, they had not yet updated their IT user list, so I had to log in as the past employee. His name appeared on my computer, every Microsoft document I opened or created—basically every work account except my email address. The name I saw everywhere, every day, was Bryan Weiss.

It was around September when the issue was corrected and everything was set up as Gina Dewink. But for months, I was Bryan Weiss by proxy.

In October of that year, I was talked into attending a group hypnotherapy session. The session was said to tap into past lives. This was a shiny, new concept to me at that point, and I shrugged and agreed to go, not having any expectations. At different times, I had tried to meditate with no luck (though this was before I understood that meditation was about repeated practice and not something achieved through luck when trying it once or twice). Plus, I'd been told in high school at a student assembly event that I was unable to be hypnotized. So I didn't expect it would work—not with a hyperactive, overanalytical mind like mine.

Yet when the past life regressionist began acquainting us with the concept, I was enthralled—smitten with the entire idea, I suppose. It was a captivating topic for a Midwestern girl raised attending Catholic church. So when the hypnotherapist mentioned the name of a pioneer in the field, I nearly jumped off my seat.

His name? Brian Weiss.

He was a Yale psychiatrist who had stumbled into past life regression and became a modern-day leader on the topic. Though it wasn't the same person, I found it bizarre that it was the same name (with just a slightly different spelling). It brought up a question I'd always pondered—are coincidences signs or directions, or are they merely random?

During that first past life regression, I ended up having a vivid, detailed, moving experience in which I was a French-Canadian man named Jean living in Quebec in the 1800s. At the end of the session, I was asked what the message was that Jean had for me, now living as Gina. In my mind, Jean turned and seemed to look inside me. With a booming, low voice, heavy with a French accent, he ordered, "Don't be afraid!"

I was shaken, yet elated. Had I received a message from a past version of myself? That seemed insane, right?

When I got home, I looked up Dr. Brian Weiss. I read every

page of his website and saw he had books for sale as well. I told everyone about my experience and my message, but back in 2016, I didn't realize it was the first day of a personal journey.

A year later, in 2017, I published a novel incorporating the idea of past lives. Before it was complete, I wrote to Dr. Weiss's secretary, asking if he would consider writing a foreword. The secretary politely declined on his behalf, but at that point, I had been to two past life regressions and was still unsure what I thought about it all. Ever the skeptic, I didn't believe it was real. Having a basic understanding of psychology and cognition, I worried some secret part of my brain thought I was failing at life, due to the alarming messages I had received from my "past selves." I wanted to comprehend where the messages were coming from, and how important they were to interpret.

But after a third past life regression, each offering a different "life" experience (though none as vivid as Jean), I realized I had changed. No matter the content of the life I viewed or the discouraging scenes I witnessed within them, I found myself less afraid of death. Less afraid in general, I suppose. More curious about the ocean of light I felt sure I'd seen and connected with after each one of these "lives" ended. And much more interested in the meaning behind having multiple lives.

Then I came across the idea of washing in the River Ganges. Where did I read about this? In a party cookbook, of all places. The book detailed the idea of a *reincarnation party*, where guests come dressed up as who they were in a previous life. The River Ganges was mentioned as a party game, though the thought struck me hard. Currently, somewhere on this Earth, people were washing themselves in a ceremony meant to stop reincarnation, to help the soul get to the highest plane and stop reliving.

With that new fascination, I started to wonder why more people didn't talk about past lives or reincarnation. I began mentioning it to people in my life just to gauge their reaction. It was usually a facial expression resembling the look people got when they witnessed a person slipping a piece of candy in their pocket while shopping—jerky, uncomfortable; unsure how to respond. What I call, the *shoplifter reaction*.

A few months later, while watching television, I saw a logo on a commercial that was two streams of swirling light. They made a symbol similar to a yin yang. It was almost the exact image I'd seen while regressed. In my vision, we were all just spheres of energy in a vast sheet of energies. And when I first joined in after leaving Earth, I swirled together with loved ones faster and faster until exploding back into the general vastness... oneness... ocean of all energies.

Seeing a real image on television that mirrored what I'd seen in my mind while regressed caused me to spend an hour online searching for any other image that looked similar. Not finding any, I ended up purchasing a necklace from a handcrafter in Russia. While it wasn't what I was looking for, it was a reminder that the idea of an energy afterworld was still very much with me, two years after my first past life regression. I had told only a handful of people about my personal vision of an afterworld. I was fifty percent sure it was my writer's imagination filling in the blanks.

But then the final push occurred as I was visiting friends in a nearby town. We made a stop at the only bookstore carrying my first book. (I didn't do a lot of brick and mortar outreach, what can I say?) My friend casually stated that she felt obligated to buy from the local establishment since we'd entered, but wasn't sure what she was in the mood to read. She said, "Maybe something will just jump out at me." And as she said that, I looked down at a helter-skelter stack of books piled up to my knee; books waiting to be sorted and put onto the shelves. Sticking out askew from the stack was just one line of text: BRIAN L. WEISS, MD.

My hand was pulling out the book before my brain could even catch up. I *had* to have it. Whether coincidence, law of attraction or some sort of destiny, it happened to be Dr. Weiss's first book that started it all: *Many Lives, Many Masters*, published in 1988 when I was just six-years old. I started reading it as soon as I got home. Thirty-nine pages in, I got goosebumps; sixty-six pages in, I stayed up late reading by the light of my cellphone far after my husband, Craig, was snoozing next to me. In the morning, I sat in my car for a spare four minutes of reading time before I had to start work. According to one of Weiss's patients while under hypnosis: we are all energy and energy is wasted on fear, therefore, we need to eradicate fear.

Don't be afraid. My first message from my first past life vision.

The seed was planted. In my Catholic days, I worried I was a nonreligious person being forcibly *called*. I'd heard Christian friends talk about their work being a *calling from God*, but I certainly wasn't the type of person to be *called* to do anything... except maybe pick up my kid from school because she was sick again. I told Craig this notion and he gave me an eyebrow raise. "Not what you signed up for?" I asked him. A headshake was all I needed. Nope. From the moment we'd started dating, we'd been clear that I was spiritual, but no longer religious and he was a former church-goer who was now agnostic. A soul search was definitely not on our life's manic agenda. But no matter the *why* behind it, I needed to understand more. In the age of endless information, I needed to know more about a soul and where it went after the body was done.

Though I'd grown up with stained glass images of what heaven was like, it was a lot to accept. In my opinion, as a Catholic, if you accepted the idea of the Biblical afterlife (you know, Heaven), you had to accept hell, demons, angels, the Virgin Mary—the list went on. By the time I reached early high school, I had left the religion. Still, my friend's favorite saying, "You can take the girl out of the Catholic church, but you can't take the Catholic *guilt* out of the girl," seemed to be true, in my case. It was a long, messy separation.

I spent a year in my early twenties visiting every church that would allow me in. I started with the ones that didn't seem all that different from my hometown church at first glance—Lutheran, Episcopalian, Methodist. From there, I moved on to the others—Assembly of God, Church of Latter-Day Saints. I chatted with believers of the Jehovah's Witnesses, Jewish and Islamic faiths, as they do not allow outsiders to attend a day of church on a whim. And at the end of my little experiment, I came up with two conclusions. One, there were far too many religions to get a taste of them all, even when the availability in southern Minnesota was narrow. Two, I came out convinced I was a believer in three vague ideas: some sort of outside force, an inner self and a "next chapter" after death... but beyond that? Unknown.

And then there was the clinical and scientific part of my brain that wanted clarification. Was there evidence? Obviously, there was and is plenty of *proclaimed* evidence. But did I believe any of it?

If I was going to embark on a personal quest to hunt down the subconscious soul, I needed to first define what I was searching for... or at least what I was hoping to find.

For the purposes of this book, I will call this otherworldly essence a soul. But just to be clear, there are many names for what I'm seeking: subconscious self, metaphysical substance, immaterial essence, animating principle, spiritual part of a person, actuating cause of an individual life, eternal self, being, spirit... the list goes on. The Bible, for example, references both a soul and a spirit.

And going back to the River Ganges, the Hindus believe the sacred power within the river's water can cleanse the soul. In fact, there is a fifty-five-day event that only occurs every twelve years called *Kumba Mela* for this very reason. Since I am a communications director at a nonprofit society with two young children at home, it's unlikely I will fly to India for the next *Kumba Mela*. But perhaps I could interview someone and learn more about Eastern religion from the comfort of my home office.

I decided to break down what I wanted to understand into sections of specialties—some I had direct access to (like a worldwide array of neurologists, thanks to my career), and others that would be a long shot (would a psychic know I was going to call her before I called?). And then, in my personal quest to become more spiritual, I would interview experts in the area and ask them: Do humans have a soul?

I began my search with the assumption we do have some sort of soul. Everyone needs a starting point, and that was mine. I believed there was some kind of intangible spirit we could not seem to quantify. So I aimed to collect interviews and opinions from a vast array of people about the concept of a soul—Christians, Hindus, mediums, hypnotherapists, neurologists, atheists, you name it. In the book *The Soul Hypothesis*, Mark Baker and Stewart Goetz observed that "most people, at most times, in most places, at most ages have believed that human beings have some kind of soul." So in that, I'm not so out of place, I suppose.

Another part of my research would be to "receive" signs; to purposely try to use the law of attraction, the pull of universal forces. I would assume for the duration of my research that if I sent the idea out there, answers would arise. Many types of people believed you could become a receiver for that type of information. And that would be my approach to this project—open to receiving signs that lead to connections. I *did* already tend to see signs that I interpreted as giving me direction, but knowing what I did about psychology, I assumed it was my brain trying to make sense out of the chaos, seeing patterns to make a kind of rationality occur where there wasn't a rational answer. (One time in 2019, Celine Dion came up in conversation like nine times in one week. I don't know what the point of such a coincidence would be... that my heart will go on?)

The day I decided to apply the concept of being open to receiving, I saw a Facebook post from a Lutheran friend proclaiming: *Ask. Believe. Receive.* A saying I had not heard before, apparently popular among those who believe in prayer and its powers. I liked the more humorous, realist way Jack Canfield put it at his seminar: *Become an AskHole.*

Okay. So I'd ask (and ask and ask). I'd be open to receiving. And I'd see where it all led me. While at the seminar, I stated three business goals I hoped to achieve. One: publish a second book. Two: join or start a business meant for women or caregivers. Three: bring more money to the household budget. I wrote these goals, said them out loud and set them aside. In the days that followed, the idea for this book bubbled up from my insides and I began to write.

Soon after beginning my soul quest and stating my intentions, I took a spontaneous trip to visit my older sister. I did not bring my children or my husband. I had not planned the weekend, nor was I working. Yet, when we went shopping at a secondhand store, I think the believers would say I *received*.

Preparing for the six-hour drive back home, I crouched down to look at the books on CD on the thrift store shelf. Though Justin Timberlake and Vampire Weekend had propelled me to Illinois, I didn't have enough music to make it back to Minnesota without dipping into our solid-gold selection of children's music or relying on the radio (which was all country and classic rock through the entire state of Wisconsin, I swear). But instead of finding an audio book to buy, a book precariously tossed on top of the row of dusty CD boxes and cassettes stared back at me. The book, called *90 Minutes in Heaven*, was a nonfiction recounting of a near-death experience. I snatched it up and purchased it, along with a cardigan and vintage green vase that would match my wallpaper at home. (Unfortunately, as a direct result of not finding a book to listen to for the next six hours, Raffi's rendition of *Banana Phone* replayed endlessly in my mind for nearly a month. Oh, you're not familiar with the song? Please. Take a google. I'll wait.)

A few days after returning to the minutiae of every day, I opened the book, not knowing a thing about it other than the title and blurb from the back cover.

I ended up reading the entire thing that day.

In sum, it was Don Piper, a Baptist preacher, explaining how he was killed in an auto accident and—while clinically dead—saw his soul arrive in Heaven. But once he returned to his human body, he had years of injuries and recovery to live through. The main message I pulled from the book was that he needed to learn to *receive*. It wasn't enough to give. Not enough to take. He had to be open to receiving—well wishes, help, assistance, you name it.

I marveled at the timing. Writing and thinking about receiving had led me to a book about spiritually receiving. Neat. It was working.

The topic bridged perfectly to the reason I stopped reading another of Brian Weiss's books, called *Messages from the Masters: Tapping into the Power of Love*. Midway through, Dr. Weiss said one of the messages from the spirit guides was that without learning how to receive, our soul was going to return to Earth to try again. His example was a woman who was a caring, active member of her community—gave to the poor, volunteered at church. At the end of her life, she fell into a vegetative state; unable to move or speak. Yet, her mind was completely normal—no brain damage or mental slowdown. Her daughter asked Dr. Weiss why something like this would happen to such a good person, as her mother had lived in that condition for years. Dr. Weiss said, via lessons he had learned from the "Masters" in the afterlife, this was to teach her to *receive* without having to come back and relive a whole other life, since she was so close to "making it."

After reading that, I got uncomfortable, stuffed in a bookmark and never went back. Having a sister with Down syndrome, I had a hard time getting into an area that could be seen as spiritual victim-blaming territory. But after taking in Don Piper's experience and his call to receive, I wondered if it was the woo-woo telling me to finish the book.

Searching for other near-death experiences opened a vast channel of information. NDEs, as they are abbreviated, have been the subject of countless books, videos, documentaries, studies, etc. But the one that I watched was done by the BBC in 2003, *The Day I Died*. It's fifty-five minutes well worth watching if interested in the topic. The documentary features interviews with both the patients who died on the surgery table (and then came back to life), as well as the surgeons in the room.

It was football season, so I watched it in bed with the tablet and headphones while Craig had the TV. The cheesy yet ominous music, coupled with the incredible content, made the hairs on my arms stand on end. (It didn't help that it was being pumped into my head in stereo, thanks to the noise-canceling headphones.)

When it ended, I ran to Craig and snuggled in under his arm for the remainder of the game instead of going to sleep as planned. The documentary showed inexplicable stories—completely impossible, in the terms used in science and medicine today. The patients interviewed made compelling and convincing points that a soul or essence had left the physical body. Those interviewed seemed able to see things in the room and hear things happening to the body while they were unconscious. Chilling.

*Taking is much different
than receiving*

The Lightworker

I MET BRINN McManus at her business after hours the week of Thanksgiving. Being Minnesota, it was already dark and frosty at 5:00pm. Despite the fact that my children, aged three and five, had knocked down our freshly-staged Christmas tree and it lay in shambles on the floor at home, I still made it a few minutes early for the interview.

I had decided to start my interviews with this woman (whom I vaguely knew from a magazine article I'd written a year earlier) for a couple reasons. First, her healing center and boutique was called *A Beautiful Soul*. Besides the on-the-nose business name, she had recently moved into a vacant building near my home. Strangely (or not strangely, if you subscribe to the school of thought that there are forces at work in the background), I had driven past the little gray building a hundred times on my drive home, always lingering an extra second on the "For Sale or Rent" sign in front, because I'd always had the urge to help it become a place of community gathering. It just had a *je ne sais quoi* that begged for a second thought from me. So when I saw what business moved in, I knew I had to go. *A Beautiful Soul* was, among other things, a community-gathering location. Just as I had wished.

When Brinn answered the door for our interview, she apologized for the disarray; she was preparing for the Christmas decorating to begin. She led me past the boutique of crystals and dreamcatchers to a back room. A Michael Jackson song was blaring and incense was burning. The room was decorated in tones of tranquil aquas and blues, the wall adorned with a painting of angel wings and a crucifix. A large statue of the Virgin Mary sat in the corner, her stone sculpted eyes watching us as Brinn asked me to take a seat.

As it was the first interview of this new adventure, I wasn't as prepared as I should have been. I only had around five questions for her. Things felt tense. I quickly realized I was walking in and asking a stranger for personal, detailed accounts of private beliefs. Could I do this? Was this too personal? Worse, was it rude?

"Tell me about *A Beautiful Soul*," I asked of her business as we sat near each other on a small sofa.

"Well, people take care of themselves in all sorts of ways," she began. "They do upkeep on their teeth, hair, clothes, yard... but what do they do for their soul?"

I smiled and shrugged a small shrug. "That's just what I'm setting out to discover. So how do you do that here?"

"I'm a lightworker who was raised as a Catholic in this lifetime," she said.

"I noticed," I said, nodding to the crucifix both on the wall and dangling around her neck.

"I have no ties to any organized religion, but I am a follower of Christ," she clarified. "I cherish so many of the practices and prayers of my upbringing. Mother Mary has always played a big part in my life. I work in service of others."

I nodded. "A lightworker? Tell me about that." At this early stage in my soul quest, I had not yet heard of a lightworker.

Brinn smiled. She was easy to talk to. "The best way I can

explain it is that we're all born in this world with this light. Imagine each of us starting our life journey holding a candle—our light. Lightworkers are born with a bouquet of 'candles' to help others find their light in the darkness when the soul is weak, tired, or ready to give up. I am a healer. I am guided to help people heal themselves and reconnect with their light within."

I nodded, wondering if Brinn knew what I needed to connect and heal.

She continued, "To many, it seems a contradiction to be a lightworker and a follower of Christ. Lightworkers know there is more. Not all lightworkers follow my path. Each goes where she is called."

"And you mentioned this lifetime," I said. "Do you believe you have lived before?"

"Yes," Brinn agreed. "I believe I've lived lives before. I discovered them through meditation and prayer. But in all of them, I've always been subservient—a midwife, a slave, another lightworker."

I couldn't believe where the universe had led me. My first interview—first step into this vast topic—and I had somehow connected with a woman raised in the Catholic Church who believed in reincarnation. Less rare then I assumed? "That's interesting," I noted. "From all of the past lives I saw of myself, I was usually a loner. I didn't seem to be serving anyone."

Brinn shook her head. I looked at Virgin Mary in the corner. I bet she, too, wanted to shake her head at my admission.

"If you believe in reincarnation, does that make you less afraid of death?" I asked the stranger sitting next to me on a sofa.

"I'm not afraid of death," Brinn said confidently.

I nodded, wondering if I would get to the point where I could answer that question so boldly.

After a few more of my meandering questions about souls and the forces and masters of the universe (which I had accidentally phrased just as in the 1980s He-Man cartoon), Brinn tossed her hand up. "It has taken me many years to become the person I am, and have the courage to share it. In sum, I try to bring the light back to souls through this healing technique; by guiding people to heal themselves. I also urge them to receive." She paused. "As an example of when people need to receive love and support without question, a story. I used to work for The American Cancer Society Hope Lodge, a free home-away-from-home for cancer patients and their caregivers. Everyone there had just one thing to do: receive."

My eyes darted up from my notes at this.

She continued, "Often, I'd hear guests saying that they couldn't possibly accept these gifts from strangers, but that was their one job," she stated, her words full of passion. "Things would happen at Hope Lodge—the laundry machines would all magically have quarters in them and that type of thing. The giving and love even followed them into the laundry room. No avoiding it. Once you begin to receive kindness and love, things change for the better. Your mood, your health, your soul," Brinn concluded.

I was nodding like a bobblehead by then. I added, "The realist in me wants to point out how often people do take, though."

Brinn shook her head. "Ah, but taking is much different than receiving. It is far more difficult to be open and vulnerable to receiving. But when you do it, you can gain so much." She sat up straighter. "When my prior landlord gave me a thirty-day notice out-of-the-blue, I couldn't fight it. I was brought here gently, without asking. People were brought into my life who changed my life. It's always hard to be humble, but we all need to receive."

After a few more moments of conversation, I stood to leave. Brinn walked me out to the main door. We wished each other a Happy Thanksgiving and I promised to keep in touch.

When I came home, brimming with new ideas, I typed them all up. I realized I needed to class up and branch out. I needed a set of actual interview questions to keep me on track (and not accidentally mimic a half-naked cartoon barbarian in front of the Virgin Mary). I also decided that if I wanted a real slice of human opinion, I would need more than southern Minnesota's perspectives. Thanks to the powers of the internet, that would be possible if I was ready to ask.

That night, I chuckled to myself that my book was turning into a metaphysical milkshake. And I liked that phrase so much, I contemplated making it the title of this book. But after a quick search, I discovered that actor Rainn Wilson had an online interview series with the same name! I wasn't sure if that was a sign or not, so I added Rainn to my potential connections list.

It was during the holiday downtime toward the end of 2018 that I fell into a rabbit hole of Facebook groups. After being invited to join one about "intuitive women in business," my group suggestions went from mundane to peculiar. It was like suddenly learning there was an entire state you had never heard of before. Some of the metaphysical groups were as large as

20,000 to 60,000 members! Groups about being an empath, becoming enlightened, soul seeking, and more.

The first group suggestion was a support group, for lack of a better term, for those identifying as empaths. Well aware of empathy, I had never heard the word used in that way. According to the members of the group, to be an empath was to feel what others felt—quite literally. Though the exact definition varied, it seemed a plight. Group members posted about ways to avoid people so as not to "soak up" negative energy and thoughts. They posted about how they could not be around people experiencing trauma because it caused them to feel the trauma symptoms as well.

Though it sounded a little paranormal (or perhaps even outrageous), I found myself nodding in agreement to many of the stories other group members shared. Since childhood, I myself *felt* what others felt. And it *did* seem like an affliction most of the time; like a weakness I carried with me. Crippled with "sympathy pains," I'd been asked to leave the classroom in health class because I was nearly crying at the explanation of how to apply a tourniquet to a wound. I was teased by my siblings for sobbing for days after watching *Titanic* because I couldn't explain it away by telling myself it was a made-up story... it had been the real lives of real people. And I mourned for them.

So after doing some reading, I had a new identifying word. I was an empath.

One group I found had an event that caught my eye—not because of the content, but because of the event image used. There it was! A near-perfect representation of the swirling energy I'd seen in the afterworld during my regression. I saved a copy of the image to my desktop and set it as my home office screensaver, and it inspired my artistic daughter to draw the "rainbow swirls," as she called them, several times.

I began using the groups as a base for finding new interviews, as well as some new perspectives. According to the seasoned veterans of the metaphysical world, I was just a cliché. A woman in her thirties going through the process of shedding an old self and beliefs and seeking a new. It was a bit off-putting and discouraging to see just how *many* others were already "past" me in my journey to understand more. There were so many people out there writing books, hosting podcasts, creating documentaries, giving readings—you name it. I realized I was stepping into the road to enlightenment and praying I didn't get hit by oncoming traffic.

Before I began my search, I thought I had a good perspective to start from because I was an "everyman." I was a moderate with equal unfamiliarity and knowledge of all sides of the conversation. I thought of myself as a blank slate with the willingness to learn. But that ended up being an isolating and depressing starting point.

I pushed through the onslaught of love and light, talk of vibrations, spirit guides, frequencies, energies... I felt overwhelmed. I couldn't get over how much the terminology was completely new to me. Considering myself a lover of learning who knew bits about many topics, it was a sting to the ego to see so much unknown. I had never heard about increasing one's vibrations or ascension markers, yet the people in these groups spoke about them as if they were recapping last night's episode of *Modern Family*. As if these were all facts they had learned about years ago.

Seeing the vast difference between the people I associated with in every day Middle America and the multicultural soul soup in the online groups, I created a survey about soul beliefs.

I sent it out into the world to my connections as well as into the groups. It was a public survey left open until the completion of the book, asking about past and current spiritual beliefs. But as of the first round, the survey results mostly just hinted at a fact I have joked about—Minnesota is the Tator Tot Hotdish of belief systems. Processed, yet homecooked with love. And being Minnesota Nice, my friends and family humored me and completed the survey in a timely fashion, even though it was most likely prompting the *shoplifter reaction* again from the other side of the computer screen.

The holidays came and went, our house filled with family, friends and germs. On Christmas night, Craig and I decided to book airline tickets to Memphis, Tennessee for our anniversary. There was a music festival he had always wanted to attend and I, being a lover of mid-century nostalgia, couldn't wait for the chance to visit Graceland. But there was more. I was curious to see if anything in Memphis would look or feel familiar, seeing as how one of my past lives was supposedly spent there as Sweet Bea, a community-minded Baptist in the 1960s. It seemed a good chance to help convince myself one way or the other (or not, because in reality, there were probably a hundred churches in Memphis. Wait, I googled it. Nineteen Baptist churches in Memphis proper. That might be doable). Either way, I was going to Memphis. It was just a bonus that it linked to my search.

By January 10, my little family was already on our third virus of the year, which made it difficult to spend time focused on the *macro* when there was so much *micro* to deal with. On top of the runny noses and whining from the wilting little ones, we'd received crushing news from the public school district. In our city, you could enter a child into an elementary school lottery that, if selected, would allow access to charter or Montessori schools at no cost—as a public school, with transportation and all. Disenchanted with our local district school and first year as school parents in general, I had placed our daughter in three school lotteries. When we received no word, we called. There were nearly 200 students on the waiting list before our daughter. She had not been selected.

Deflated and full of Mama Bear wrath, I vowed to several people that I would do whatever it took to get my brilliant young daughter into a better school, including moving (even though we'd only been in our current house for less than three years). I spent time looking into community programs and other ways to supplement her education. I pored over the tight housing market, increasing interest rates, fluctuating school district lines, school rankings—I was obsessed. And after the back and forth and pros and cons, we concluded doing nothing was our best option at that point with all things considered (#MomFail).

Through the family drama, I'd still managed to do some reading over the holiday break, and set up a few more interviews. In the spirit of yin and yang, I was craving a differing opinion to my newfound headful of love and light. I picked up the project again by talking to a neurologist from Italy. After selecting a time that worked in each of our time zones, I called him on my cell phone to conduct the interview. This time, I had sent him the interview questions beforehand. I had fifteen thoughtful questions for him, ranging from his medical perspective to his personal. But when I tried to call him, I discovered my cell phone would not make long-distance calls to another country! After a flurry of emails back and forth, we canceled the interview. Again, I questioned what the heck I was doing. I was juggling a stressful part-time job, hands-on care for two small children (which included daily drop-offs and pick-ups at both a preschool and a kindergarten), freelance projects ranging from magazine articles to website redesigns and the general rest of life.

But my husband, Craig—ever my rock—simply asked, "Why don't you just video chat?"

And behold, there were more interviews.

It's simply the net calculation of all micro synaptic activity

The Neurologist

Liborio Parrino, MD is an Associate Professor of Neurology at Parma University in Italy. Dr. Parrino began his career by studying the recovery of sleep in comatose patients. Thirty-five years later, he continues to work in the field of sleep medicine and research. I reached out to Dr. Parrino because as a neurologist who's worked with people in a coma, I thought he may have some rare experiences and interest in the topic of a soul.

The time we settled on for the interview was 8:00am, my time. This meant for my cross-continental conversation, I had exactly twenty minutes between getting ready for work and getting the kids bundled in coats, hats and mittens to walk to the school bus stop.

After bribing the kids to leave me alone, I began by explaining my project to Dr. Parrino, computer to computer. Sucking in a breath, I dove right in. "If out-of-body experiences or visions of an afterlife are *not* real, is there a physical portion of the brain that might be responsible for creating them?"

"Hippocampal cortex in the limbic system," was his answer, spoken with expertise and an Italian accent. A search revealed the limbic system is the supporter of functions such as long-term memory, behaviors and emotions.

He continued his thought, "Or perhaps the parietal

lobe—sensations and perceptions. The subcortex does cognitive mapping. In more complex cases, perhaps in the brain stem or multiple cortical regions."

I was scribbling as fast as I could, making a note to myself not to begin an interview with so many complicated terms. Though the exact part of the brain that may have been responsible for creating these "past lives" wasn't as important as I had first deemed, I was just relieved to hear that there was, indeed, a portion of the brain that I could finger-point as the culprit.

When I looked back to the computer screen, Dr. Parrino's computer camera was on, but it was pointed at the ceiling. It was around 3:00pm in Italy and the sterile white appearance of the ceiling and wall disclosed he was in a hospital setting.

I changed directions quickly, not wanting to waste his time. "Have you ever watched a patient's body die?" I asked, pen ready to write as quickly as he spoke. "And if yes, did you view anything that could be evidence of a soul?"

"Unfortunately," he began, "I have seen many. In Italy, three medical professionals are required to declare a patient dead—a neurologist to declare cerebral death, a medical doctor and an intensive care specialist. Many times, I have stared into those eyes," he told me. "Those dead eyes looking at somewhere—the ceiling or sky. I always try to decide if there's still life. Is death when all organs are out of action? It's a strange sensation to declare someone legally dead. Oddly, I have noticed that the physicians who watch patients die often want to eat right after. Peculiar to me."

I agreed it was peculiar, thinking back to articles I had read about how many people have a strong desire to eat or engage in sexual activities after attending a funeral—the theory being 'because they are still alive.' Perhaps it was a similar subconscious tendency for physicians? I continued on. "So in your experiences, have you ever witnessed anything unexplainable within a patient's brain that might hint to a soul?"

"Unexplainable? No."

I felt my shoulders deflate a bit.

Dr. Parrino continued, "There are really no unexpected surprises. An EEG may show fragments of neuro-networks that survive. So perhaps we are never absolutely sure every part is dead."

"So the fragments in the brain that you say are visible on an EEG after a patient is declared dead—could that be construed as evidence of a soul?"

Dr. Parrino chuckled. "You reminded me of the Dan Brown book, *The Lost Symbol*, when they weigh the body before and after death to see if a soul has a weight to it—microelements."

"Then you believe humans have a soul?" I was still taking notes to look up the Dan Brown novel, assuming I knew where the conversation was headed. I'd assumed wrong.

"No," Dr. Parrino stated, the confidence in his answer shocking to a wavering mind such as mine. "I do not believe humans have a soul. It's simply the net calculation of all micro synaptic activity. Perhaps there's a soul of the universe—a mysterious big brother living in the universe somewhere—but not in humans. All the pieces composing a body are free to run back after death. Back to some untraceable position in the universe. Our molecules run back into the water, the ground, the air, trees, animals. Life is a nonentropic caveat."

My hands were flying, but I took the time to underline that statement. It was deep and I wanted to pick it apart. It seemed he was using nonentropic to mean changing from a state of disorder to order. Caveat meaning a warning that there were certain conditions present in what one was about to agree to. What a well-stated definition of life.

Dr. Parrino continued, "Degradation rather than order. Once a body dies, physics take over. Death is natural. If you accept life, you accept death. It's physics, not something mental. Cognition is proportional to molecules. The molecules will disperse again after death—maybe some in a dog, some in an apple, some in a television—who knows."

"So in some ways, you believe in reincarnation?" I poked.

He chuckled again. "In those two or three million molecules inside an apple, perhaps."

"When you were young, were you raised in any certain religion?"

"In the United States, I attended a Catholic school in Brooklyn, New York until the age of ten. I continued to follow actively the Catholic religion until I was twenty-five."

"In much of my searching, I've found many who believe there is fate or collective conscious guiding us. What are your thoughts about that?" I asked.

"I believe genius is the best expression of the whole," Dr. Parrino told me. "To look at a genius, yes, she may be a true genius, but she is the multiplication and sum of all the people living at that point in life. Whether it be tech science now or painters of the past. It is a sum of the environment and culture, never a single self, but an orchestra of selves."

Another underline. An orchestra of selves—a beautiful way to explain the human collective.

"But as far as fate, "Dr. Parrino continued, "There is the same fate for us all."

I looked up, eager for his explanation. "What fate is that?"

"That we will live in magic for our forty, sixty or eighty years and then move to natural, entropic degradation. We all have this life given to us. Perhaps by that big brother. We all have years of possibilities."

A smile spread across my face, but a glance at the time kept me from engaging in that thought. "In general, would you say you are afraid of death?" I asked, too brisk for my liking.

Dr. Parrino didn't hesitate. "I'm afraid of pain and death that is often related to a suffering framework. Beyond those constraints, I'm basically not afraid of death," he replied.

I was enjoying our conversation, but a cry from the other room pulled me back to real life. I asked the final question. "In your life, have you ever had any metaphysical or otherworldly experiences of note?"

Without hesitation, he again answered in his definitive tone. "No. Not in the way you mean. But in my many years of studying sleep, I know that every one of us experiences other-worldly magic on a nightly basis."

"We do?"

I could hear a smile in his voice. "It is dreaming. To sleep offers more opportunities to dream, in which we can encounter the most marvelous of experiences."

His words were so beautiful. I felt just the same about dreaming, always having had very vivid ones. With a smile on my face, I finished our interview. "Thank you so much for your time and experience, Dr. Parrino."

With a seasoned neurologist's point of view rattling around in my mind for the next few days, I started to wonder if there was a scientific answer to every question. Science seemed like inexplicable magic to the untrained brain, yet physics could supply an answer to so many human quandaries. Plus, thinking about grandpa's molecules in an apple somewhere was a visual that stuck with a person.

In the direction of learning more about the scientific side of beliefs, I reached out to the Humanists of Minnesota, the Center for Inquiry and the Atheist Speakers Bureau to set up more interviews.

While I was sending out asks to those who likely did not believe in a soul, I was receiving more and more mysticism from those who did. My Facebook group suggestions had tripled in size. And they were all pointing to the strange reality that individuals looking to learn about this topic did somehow find each other and connect. Everyone on any sort of spiritual enlightenment journey was joining together to pose questions like, "What happens after a body dies?" and "What is a soul?" and "What level of ascension are you living on?" Through a post on a group dedicated to Practical Mysticism (which many members outed as an oxymoron), I read a comment that seemed like it was an answer to my major question—did our souls live more than once? It was made by a woman in India who looked close to my age. I reached out and hoped for a positive reply. In the meantime, I began my research on Eastern religions.

Reincarnation

D ID YOU KNOW Hinduism is the third largest religion in the world? I certainly didn't. It's estimated that more than a billion (yes, with a 'b') individuals identify their religion as Hindu. Yet here in the billowing corn fields of the Midwest, I had a hard time coming up with one to talk to. Since Hindus believe in past lives, I thought I should hear from someone brought up in the faith, rather than what I could read.

From what I could gather, Hindus have no prophet, no church, no higher human authorities to follow at all. As the oldest religion on Earth (so scholars say), the concept sounded like one lost in the mayhem of our human history. They do believe in a universal soul (God) called *Brahman*, so we have that idea in common. As a set of life examples to follow, I had to admit, it didn't sound too bad—especially compared to the regulation and punishment system indoctrinated into my mind from the Catholics. It seems most Hindus have four goals to achieve in life. They are tasked with stopping their soul from reincarnating, to unite with the universal soul (Brahman); following 'nature's law,' called Dharma; achieving material gain without harming anyone else (Artha); and using a Karma system.

Dharma was a bit difficult for me to grasp as a concept without examples. The dharma of water is to flow. The dharma of a tiger is to hunt. Apparently, even karmic exchanges are examples of dharma.

I went to see a hypnotherapist in southern Minnesota and she led a hypnotherapy session to regress us to view our past lives without even seeming sure she *believed* in past lives. Now, to be fair, I've completed four sessions and viewed four past lives and I still haven't decided if I believe it was my subconscious, dream-mind making up stories, or if I was accessing actual memories stored away up there. But I bet if I were Hindu, there would be no question. At least, that's what I assumed before learning more about dharma. When I later questioned someone raised in India, she explained, "Our emphasis has always been on 'seeking' from own experience, rather than knowing from books. We have been taught in our homes and community—from our ancestors—that there are different paths to reach the ultimate, and that's what different religions or no religion or atheism means. We must explore and wonder about our own discoveries. 'My' experience is 'my' primary knowledge and what we 'have been told' is secondary. There is a big difference between falling in love and reading about others falling in love."

Perhaps that's the key for me. I experienced clear, vivid scenes. I fell in love. And the part of the past life process I've spent the most time pondering is the immediate answers. Like a seasoned pro on the set of *Jeopardy,* my brain is able to answer the questions asked by the hypnotherapist in split-second time.

What are you wearing? Are you married? Do you have children?

Every time, I got answers in the voice of the person I was viewing. Though I've written pages on each experience (Appendix B), here are the quick synopses.

First, I saw Jean (male), as I mentioned. He was a trapper

and fur trader living in Quebec, Canada with his wife, Marie, and daughter. From the type of clothes and rifle, I figured it to be around 1850 to 1890. I spoke French and lived a quiet, happy life. The main point Jean wanted to tell me was, "Don't be afraid." He died alone in his cabin of some disease that caused him to cough up blood.

Next, about six months after that, I saw Vinny (male). He was an Italian immigrant living alone in Brooklyn in around 1910. He was macho, and boxed opponents in the alley to make an extra buck. I saw him hanging out with a crowd of other iron workers at Daube's bar night after night, after working on a skyscraper. He died because, instead of asking for help moving huge 'flour sacks' of concrete, he tried to lift two at once, flung them over his shoulder, lost his balance, tipped backward and fell down an open elevator shaft. His message was, "Well, this was a wasted life." He was only around twenty years old.

Then in 2018, I went back and met Sweet Bea (female). A wonderful, gregarious black woman living in Memphis in the 1960s. (The first female I had viewed.) Sweet Bea was working as a housekeeper, had a daughter she adored and a son in jail. She was active in her Baptist church, boisterous and well-loved. She was working on equal rights when she suddenly died in her fifties of a heart attack (or maybe a brain aneurysm) while baking cookies for a big to-do in the community. Her message was that she felt we'd gotten closer to what we needed to be—a supportive community member, a loving mother, a civil rights activist—but life had ended too soon.

I went to my fourth regression almost hoping for a chink in the time chain. I decided that unless the life I saw was older than 1850, my mind was just making this all up because the timeline wouldn't work out. Because how could I be alive as two different people at the same point in time? And my lives from Jean up to Gina were packed in there.

More than anything, I wanted understanding. Was my imagination creating stories while in a meditative state? If yes, was there a pattern to the messages? Was there still a message that needed to be gleaned?

During that fourth session, I had a more difficult time "going under" and getting to that space in my mind where I watched lives play out like movies. I saw snips of two other lives—almost as if channel-surfing—before dropping in on Gregory Smythe, a wealthy banker and businessman living in Liverpool in 1792.

Needless to say, the timeline worked. And I was left knowing that either I lived and failed many lives before this one, or that my subconscious thought I was failing at my current life and felt the need to keep telling me so. If you included my current life as Gina, born in 1982, that lends five experiences to pull from. And in two out of five, I had completely avoided connecting with people. In a majority of lives, I was hovering in a neutral zone—not seeming to have done anything decidedly good or evil. In the last vision, Gregory was a single man who worshiped the freedom to do as he pleased. He boarded a ship to explore a different continent—Africa, perhaps—and died of yellow fever while there. With no heirs or even friends, no one knew or cared about his death. His message to me was that "freedom is *not* more important than love." I kept seeing him shaking his head, completely despondent, muttering how sorry he was for wasting another life.

Throughout my life, people have called me an old soul. But while I had always taken that as a compliment, I was starting to wonder if it meant I kept flunking out of *life school* and being sent back to retake the test.

Dr. Brian Weiss interviewed thousands of individuals while they were under hypnosis. He collected what he calls "messages from the masters" because so many of the tales he recorded had similarities in what people viewed after the past life session ended and the soul went to the spirit world. When he compiled the stories, he claimed to have discovered that there were seven "levels" souls must pass through. (Which immediately made me envision Will Ferrell describing the seven levels of the Candy Cane Forest in *Elf*.)

After a search in my Facebook groups, I saw that the ascension levels were a concept very alive with some. And there were, in fact, seven that people referred to. Though a picture on the internet was not what I was aiming to use as a reference, when I asked where more information could be found on the topic, no one seemed to know where to lead me, other than to meditation.

If reincarnation was real and I was reliving over and over, shouldn't I be concerned about how safe and neutral I was playing it in this life? I found a group of people who were living "in 5 D," which was one of the ascension levels. I joined to watch the conversations. It was obvious that many people in the group had been raised in an Eastern religion.

It prompted me to seek out a temple in the area. One I had driven past, seeing it surrounded by miles of farmland and homesteads, peeking out as a jarring contrast of red, white and gold. A Cambodian Buddhist Temple, Watt Munisotaram, that welcomed tours and questions on its forty-acre campus. I made a plan to visit the temple in the spring. From the website, I found there were resident Buddhist monks, as well as board officials. I was hopeful someone would agree to be included in my project, as I always learn better directly from another human.

The more I looked into other religions, the more days I spent lost in webpages and books. One led to the next in an ever-growing cycle of information. Understanding more about reincarnation led to Hinduism, which let to Buddhism. And Hinduism and Buddhism were difficult for me; all the unfamiliar words and terminology. I felt like I needed to register for a class just to understand the basics. Though I'd heard in passing about Buddha, the *Tibetan Book of the Dead* and Nirvana, I did not know how deeply rooted these concepts were. It reminded me of the movie *Idiocracy* when "common sense" knowledge was forgotten through generational games of *Telephone*.

I lived a few days obsessed with the fact that there were about a billion people out there who would tell me my past lives were real; that I was a fool to even question it (though the basic definition of what was reincarnated would still be varied).

My soul quest went deeper than I intended.

I stumbled upon an image of "Bhavacakra" that stopped me short. Buddhists were so sure of a cyclical existence that they had visual aids to assist in teaching. Within the explanation of the image, I read the following:

> *"Ringu Tulku states: We create karma in three*
> *different ways, through actions that are positive,*
> *negative, or neutral. When we feel kindness and love*
> *and with this attitude do good things, which are*
> *beneficial to both ourselves and others, this is positive*
> *action. When we commit harmful deeds out of equally*

harmful intentions, this is negative action. Finally, when our motivation is indifferent and our deeds are neither harmful or beneficial, this is neutral action. The results we experience will accord with the quality of our actions."

Neutral experiences bring neutral results? Around and around the wheel I go with no ending? Well, that could explain why I was always so tired...

There are many, many heavens
and many, many places we can be

The Hindu

WHEN I WAS able to set up a video chat with Pooja Mamgain, the woman from India I'd met through an online group, I was thrilled to finally have a human resource to ask about reincarnation. I had stockpiled a backlog of questions. Pooja agreed to call me at 9:30pm on a Sunday, which was 10:00am for me. Through our laptops, I could see she was seated on a couch covered in a white cloth with blue butterflies and birch trees. She rested against a bright pink pillow with a green tree sprawling out from the center. She had an easy, friendly smile.

"I am Pooja," she started when I asked for an introduction. "I have a Master's in Environment Science and Urban Environment Law and have spent most of my life studying and practicing Eastern Religion."

I thanked her for agreeing to give up time on a Sunday and explained the aim of my book. She was instantly personal.

"I have experiences to share and look for people to share them with, but I will tell you things that no one else knows," she said sincerely. "Because you asked. No one has asked me before."

"Thank you," I replied. "That is very kind." I blushed.

"We are connected. We are friends," she told me, which opened up our conversation and its possibilities right away.

With a smile on my face, I asked her to describe her religious background and beliefs.

"I was born to a Hindu Brahmin family at the foothill of the Himalayas. You would say I was brought up in a Hindu family, but there are no restrictions here. Many different cultures come together in India and we do not have rules about them. We all have individual beliefs. It was not until I was eighteen that we discussed these topics. There are many spiritual figures. In history, those living between one geographic region and another were told, 'You are Hindu.' We said, 'Okay.' It is more like a branding," she finished with a small laugh.

I nodded and took notes, asking next about her own personal experiences that led to her belief system.

"I grew up learning Indian philosophies, yoga, stories from our epics, attending discourses and reading philosophy books. When I was sixteen," she began, leaning forward toward the camera, "I started meditation. I am thirty-one now. It is a large part of my life. I am now able to meditate for up to eight hours."

I couldn't keep the shock out of my expression. The idea of meditating for an entire workday made me twitchy.

"I have had many, many experiences," Pooja recalled. "I never used to think all of this was practical before. This topic was just not practical to me. But now I see that everything is practical. Now it is simple. Meditation is a simple, practical part of life. We see the universe, and that is practical. How could we not learn from our ancestors? After meditation comes into practice, everything seems so simple and practical."

I couldn't help but think back to my *Idiocracy* comparison in my own mind. Sitting still and doing nothing. Being bored until past the boredom. Such an uncomplicated concept, now mostly lost. People made appointments for that now; carved time out of hectic schedules so they could sit on fancy mats in designer pants for the chance to do nothing. Maybe it didn't need to be that calculated? Perhaps it was a skill we all should hone. I had never meditated, other than the hypnotherapy sessions, and wasn't even sure if those counted. "So you have experienced your past lives while meditating?" I clarified.

"Many, many," Pooja recounted. "I've gone so far, I have seen myself as a fish... A fish with my arm cut off! I have seen twenty or thirty lives. One, in Europe, where I saw my sister. I believe we chose to live together again—to share lives together. And in one, I was alive in 1990! But I was Pooja in 1990; born in 1988. If you find an explanation to this, you must tell me. I am left to assume time is not linear."

My mind went over my personal past life timeline. It was extremely close between one death and another birth. And I had assumed overlapping timelines meant it was all made up in my mind. Pooja had come to a completely different conclusion when faced with the same dilemma. Maybe time wasn't linear after Earth?

"I spoke with an astrologer once," Pooja continued, "who said I have been very, very bad to men. He told me I tortured my father and was not fair to men in past lives. This was because men were bad to me. So in this life, I chose a life with few men. I have three sisters and my mother. My father expired when I was eight. I chose this life because of my past life experiences."

"So you do believe we get to choose which life we go into next?" I asked, knowing it was a common ideology that came with the past life belief.

"Yes," she answered with ease.

"And what, do you think, is the reason for choosing this life?"

Pooja paused for the first time in her effortless explanations. Then she picked up with just as much energy as before. "The lesson is to have compassion for people. Compassion for people who are angry, because we were once angry. To know 'I have also been in that place. I have been a murderer. I have been the worst of things' and to not call them a devilish fiend, but to forgive them as you forgave yourself. Many fears in this life are tied to fears from past lives. I am respectful of this decision to live this life. I do not regret it and I am grateful."

Her words sounded like a love sonnet meant for every human to hear. I was thankful she had agreed to be interviewed. "You are grateful you have chosen this life?" I reiterated.

"I am grateful to experience." She sat back a bit in her chair and let out a small chuckle. "I will share with you something I have not shared with anyone. Again, because they did not ask me. And you did."

Her words made me feel unworthy of the secret that was coming.

Pooja put her hands up in a gesture like holding a globe. "Three times when I was meditating, my body was not there." Her hands swiped across one another and her head shook at her own statement. "It is difficult to put into words, but I had no feelings or things coming from me. In that state, I had nothing. I was nothing. I didn't even know to *know* that I didn't have a body. That may sound like being a piece of furniture, but it was not like being a piece of furniture!" She paused to laugh and put her hands in her lap. "That state changed my life," she told me. "In this life, I have had doubts and depression; I have wept. But I have realized that those things are still better than *that* state of being. We came here for experiences. And we can experience *so much* in life." She looked to the side and smiled her pretty smile. "I have not left my makeup or watching movies or any of that. I just enjoy *more* now. Life is better... but it feels very tiring."

Again, I was wowed that Pooja had hit on that exact thought I'd had. Perhaps our exhaustion was related to living and learning so much.

"Life is circular, not linear," Pooja told me as if this was a well-researched fact. "Meditation and past life regressions are experiences that are real. They are real because we go there and heal there. But when we come back here, the healing and changes still exist. For example, if a child burns his hand, he learns from that experience before talking words. He will know not to touch the hot dish again even before anyone tells him so. Even if there's suffering, we are very lucky to experience joy and tears and fears." She nodded to herself, then looked to the side; picturing something in her mind. "I have seen that stage three times," Pooja said again. "I cannot decipher if it is here or somewhere else. But from being in that stage, I am sure we are here to experience."

I nodded in agreement. "Have you had any other experiences that have formed your soul beliefs?" I asked, my hand on page four of taking notes. Pooja was sure and knowledgeable. She also held emotion and conviction when explaining her practices. I was eager to hear more.

"Yes. I have connected," she stated, taking a moment to push back her soft, black hair. "After two months of maintaining noble silence, my hands began sending me signals." She interjected, "Noble silence is also a meditation, but has its individual importance. We stay in isolation and don't speak or listen to anyone, don't read or write; all we do is just be with ourselves and our thoughts for the entire time." She went back to explaining her original thought. "Language is difficult for the universe, but symbols and music can connect energies. I could not believe it when my hands began talking to my brain using mudras. Do you know mudras?"

"I am aware of them, but no, I do not know much about them," I admitted.

"After I realized my hand was talking to myself, I was not afraid at all," Pooja explained, getting far more excited. "I felt so connected to energy. I begged to type something or write something, but I could not. The mudras were all that came to me; all natural symbols, like infinity symbol, planetary motions. The message was that 'it's already there.' Symbols are in the flower patterns, the way the petals are arranged, the way the planets move. It's all natural. Over twenty days, I got forty or fifty symbols… can I show you my journal?" She asked, snapping me out of my trance.

My mind was imagining the infinity ring of flower petals that encircle its center, something I *had* actually thought about before. "Yes, please, I would love to see," I told her.

She jumped up from the couch, leaving her bright pink pillow to stare back from the other side of the world. (Literally. I later showed my five-year-old which part of the world I was talking to and she noted it was about half of the map away.)

When Pooja came back after a moment, she held up a pencil drawing she had created. It was a crude scribbling at first glance, but it was mesmerizing. It reminded me of images I'd seen from people who created art in their sleep, or while speaking in tongues or under hypnosis. My interpretation of her picture was that it was a galaxy with the infinity symbol over it, right in the middle. The background galaxy was startlingly similar to the yin yang-like symbol I'd been searching for when

I purchased that necklace while under the influence of red wine and deep thoughts.

"I have more than one hundred of these," she told me, lowering the journal page to set the camera back on her face. "I receive symbols with my... with my dancing hands!" she said lightly. "But I have a friend who receives them in a different manner. He told me his spirit guide asked him to find the chakras of the earth. You know about chakras, yes?"

"Yes," I answered, scribbling like mad to keep up with the unfolding story. "But I didn't know the Earth had any."

"He found a website of the different countries; of Mother Earth's chakras," Pooja explained. "It led us to understand that there are chakras in all. There are microchakras—your eyes have chakras, your nose." She pointed to each. "There are chakras of Earth and even of the solar system. Here we meditate a lot," she stated, referring to her area in India. "Often people are like... *Que Sera Sera*," she explained with a laugh. I loved her use of the phrase, as it had been my daughter's favorite lullaby, and indeed words I tried to live by. "People are often saying things like, 'We'll see.' This makes sense because of our geographic location—our chakra here. We have good energy. You can find a map of all of the important heritage sites, and they fall on certain chakras," Pooja told me, making me yearn to start an image search. Where would the United States fall on that chakra map?

Pooja and I continued talking for over an hour. It was an enchanting experience. She talked about deities, past life stories, auras and hearing celestial music. My final question for her was personal, as most of my questions were. "So if you believe in reincarnation, in karma, in this other plane of existence where we cannot experience anything—then do you believe in a heaven? Is there an end to the circle?"

She started making the infinity symbol in the air with her finger. "There are many, many heavens and many, many places humans can be. Perhaps we get very tired and we rest, but we choose to come back. We seem to keep coming back. We just want to *be*." She paused. "I feel good about it. We have come for these experiences. We must enjoy them."

We ended the call agreeing we were now friends. I promised to keep learning and she promised to send me more information. She also suggested I look into a 2,000-page book called *The Great Chronicle Of Buddhas*.

After my interview with Pooja, she kept her promise and emailed me several references. I kept mine and learned more about Earth's chakras.

The most common belief states chakras are seven major psychological energy centers running along the human spine. From there, chakras are related to the Earth. From what I could find, Pooja's area in India was about 200 miles from an energy center located in Mount Kailash, Tibet—the crown. The Crown Chakra is believed to be the connection to the universe; the highest chakra, the seventh chakra—literally the top. Meanwhile, Minnesota was around 1,950 miles from the nearest Earth chakra, Mount Shasta in California. That location is considered to be the Root Chakra, which symbolized a connection to the physical world or Mother Nature. It also happens to be chakra number one... the beginning, the lowest, the starting point. An interesting concept to ponder.

At that time in Minnesota, we *were* pretty connected to Mother Nature. The weather had dipped into a "polar vortex" with temperatures as low as -45°F. Schools were canceled across the state from Monday through Thursday. On the outside, it looked like a great time to schedule interviews and curl up with one of the many books I purchased for my Soul 101 semester (which remained piled and unopened in my home office), but in reality, my children were restless, my day job was busy, and trying to leave the house was impossible. To make matters worse, the internet cable going to our house emerged from the frozen ground—then had several inches of snow dumped on it, then was rained on, then froze into a giant ice mound. I was forced to cancel the few interviews I had set up due to the patchy, intermittent internet service. (Yes, a first-world problem, I'll be first to admit; thankful we have internet in the first place.)

With cabin fever hot on my frozen heels, I spent a shameful amount of time surfing the online groups I had joined. But the weight of the ever-heavy conversations wore me down. Like so many people my age, I viewed Facebook as a mindless escape. A bad habit, really. It was like feeding my brain candy instead of a healthy meal (a turn of phrase learned from positive speaker Jim Rohn), and I wanted more sugar all the time. But opening the feed to read about death and living a meaningful life and the power of living in the *now* was not candy. So I left a couple of the more intense groups and went back to *liking* baby pictures posted by my drinking-buddies-turned-parents instead.

As the winter wore on (and the news reminded us it was the coldest it had been since 1996), social media began congratulating us for surviving the "year" of January. There was the Marie Kondo craze that overtook my feed, since we were all stuck in the house and unable to leave. Even my five-year-old daughter spent an afternoon folding her clothes into squares and lining her drawer with vertical leggings.

February came. Craig and I were able to find a babysitter and escape to a work dinner party my coworker was hosting on Groundhog's Day. A new coworker in her early twenties made a comment that the movie *Groundhog Day* was the most depressing movie she had ever seen. Her boyfriend laughed and chimed in, "Only because she always falls asleep and has never seen the ending!" The conversation struck me because it mirrored much of my own secret opinions on reincarnation. What a hopeless, never-ending cycle it seemed... but was that because I had yet to see the ending? Pooja and a consensus online believed a person got to choose whether they returned to live again or not. But that seemed very convenient. I wondered how many would come back if given the choice. Would I? Had I?

The day after the work party was the Super Bowl. With Craig gone for the night and the kids tucked in, I snuggled up with a blanket and pulled out one of my dad's old VHS videos: *Cocoon*. Most of my childhood had been spent watching movies and reading books. My father had always had an extensive collection of both. I borrowed *Cocoon* and an old Jerry Lewis movie to revel a bit in the past, a beloved pastime of mine.

Curling up with popcorn and hitting play on the VCR we still had hooked up in the basement, I told myself it was more for research than for Steve Guttenberg in short shorts. Sure enough, at the end of the movie when the senior citizens decided to leave, spending eternity somewhere else, it seemed a metaphor for reincarnation. In turn, that reminded me of the Albert Brooks movie, *Defending Your Life*, in which Brooks has a life review after death. That made me think of the cult classic, *Second Sight* with Bronson Pinchott (you know, Balki) in which Pinchott has the ability to communicate with the afterworld. Maybe the 1980s were going through a soul crisis as well. I couldn't recall another decade of films that referenced so much afterlife theory. (Side note: maybe watching all of those movies as an impressionable young child was the reason I felt so compelled to be on this soul quest in the first place.)

After making the observation about pop culture in the 1980s, I did notice a small rash of "afterlife" shows pop up on the what-to-watch-next queue: *The Good Place*, *Miracle Workers* and *Good Omens*. So maybe the 1980s were when seeds were planted and now the thirty-somethings were curating the plant life of new semi-spiritual content.

Whether it was a coincidence or woo-woo, but the day after writing about 1980s movies, the main song from *Second Sight* came on the radio: Aretha Franklin singing *Freeway Of Love*. Do you often hear this song on the radio? I don't...

Synchronicity just is.
It's not a sign.

The Psychologist

WITH A SHORT intermission from weather small talk, I received a declination for an interview, only my second thus far. It was from a devout Jehovah's Witness. He preferred to not be interviewed, but asked me to read the Bible in lieu of speaking with him. I thanked him for his time.

This led up to the fifth 'no school' snow day of the year and a chance to meet with a psychologist living in Austria.

Dr. Brigitte Holzinger is a psychologist and psychotherapist from Austria. She is also the Director of the Institute for Consciousness and Dream Research, with a strong background in lucid dreams. I reached out to her to ask if she would like to be interviewed as part of my project. Also a writer, she emailed back telling me about her own books, which cover the topics of sleep, nightmares and lucid dreaming respectively.

When we were able to talk over Skype, both children were home. *Moana* was playing in the next room, and I had transformed myself from snow-day-with-the-kids mom to working professional by adding eye liner and a business-casual shirt.

Dr. Holzinger answered my call over the computer without video, but we were able to hold a pleasant conversation.

Since she had received my interview questions in advance, I

explained the premise for my book and thanked her for partic-ipating.

I was eager to hear from a psychologist on the topic. "If someone had a very vivid out-of-body experience, what might be a psychological way of explaining the experience? Do we know?" I asked.

In her Austrian accent, Dr. Holzinger explained, "The psy-chological way to explain this is disassociation, which is when there is too much pain, and a person is unable to bear it. Simi-lar to multiple personality disorder, the theory is that by disas-sociating from one's self, they can be spared some of the pain."

I knew one of my upcoming interviews was with a person who had nearly died and experienced something unexplain-able. It also made me think of the pastor from *90 Minutes in Heaven*, who had been in more pain that I knew a human could endure. I continued with my questions. "Do you think if these experiences were made up in the mind that they are still important messages for the person to process?"

"Particularly for experiences that are meaningful and important, I see people often don't share them or speak of them. They think, 'Who could relate to this experience?' and don't want to be psychologized. Is it a valuable experience? Experiences such as these, such as precognitive dreams, are hard to prove. Like the way people have dreams about events that later happen. Some of my colleagues say such a thing needs special attention, but I believe it's quite common. I have seen it in my dream research."

"So in your research and your psychotherapy, have you encountered past life experiences? Do you believe in past lives?"

"I have had patients talk about past life experiences, yes, but that's not the area I work in. I work in the here and now.

I don't fully disregard it; I listen carefully. It's... what's the phrase? New age-y," she described. "Though I know of one school using a therapy to make people hyperventilate and hallucinate. These patients often perceive what they call past lives, but I do not know—it could be fantasy. No matter, it is impressive for them. It is an important experience for them."

Steering the conversation to a different vein, I asked, "What is your psychological explanation for the prominence of holding strong spiritual or metaphysical beliefs?"

Dr. Holzinger took a moment to organize her thoughts. "My answer to that is twofold. The psychotherapist's opinion might quote Marx. You know this quote? *Religion is the opium of the people?*"

"Yes, I'm familiar."

"Religion can offer an escape from current life. But that doesn't mean I'd take away anyone's beliefs. If religious beliefs are not helping someone run away, in my opinion, it is very enriching, and therefore, why take it away from anyone?" She paused. "Although, I have colleagues who view it as a means to help wars happen. If there weren't fanatics, there wouldn't be wars—that side of things."

I nodded, writing every word with a pen on my yellow notepad.

She continued, "Many people with spiritual experiences have them when they need uplifting. They are helpful in times of pain or loss. So I say, who is a psychologist to say no?"

"Do you believe that humans have a soul?"

"A soul..." she mused. "I... I don't know. I have not thought about it enough. Yes, I've lost people and thought about it then, but at that point, you are in a different state of mind. You can have impressions of things happening, but who knows if it really is... though I hope it is."

"So are you afraid of death then, without being sure we have souls?" I asked, again feeling awkward to ask a stranger such a deeply personal question.

"I'm one of those people who hopes to live until 120!" she declared with a small laugh. "I hope it doesn't take me soon. I'm under the impression that people who die at a certain age have reached completion or tiredness. Like a sense that it's okay enough to leave existence. I have heard people say, 'I have had a very full life and it would be okay if I have to leave.' Like a friend of a colleague," Dr. Holzinger began in a solemn tone. "She had an incurable disease. She brought herself to terms with parting. In Switzerland, they have clinics that will kill you—it costs a lot, but if you reach the qualifications and prove your illness is difficult and there is nothing you can do, you can have it done."

My eyes were wide. "I did not know places like that existed. That would be illegal here in the United States."

"Yes, illegal in most places," she agreed. "Perhaps it is also legal in the Netherlands? You must look this up. I believe the clinic gives a lethal injection. The person can choose to have friends and family around. From what I heard, it is painless and mostly self-determined."

We were both quiet for a moment. It almost felt like a moment of silence for those who have had to face such a decision. I picked up again. "Do you believe the universe or destiny or some sort of collective conscious is able to guide people with signs or signals?"

She paused. "Everything has rhythms and is communicating. Biological rhythms. Existence is moving along in rhythms, and I wouldn't call it coincidence. Synchronicity just is. It's not a sign."

We finished our interview with her discussing a research

paper she had attempted to have published regarding lucid dreams and telepathic dreams that, though impressive, was rejected by the psychology journal, reminding me that the entire topic was often seen as "fringe."

After Dr. Holzinger and I hung up, I looked up synchronicity. I knew the term, but wanted a definition.

The concept of synchronicity from psychologist Carl Jung stated that events were meaningful coincidences, or instances of synchronicity, if they occurred with no relationship, but seemed related. As I had guessed, the concept of synchronicity as more than mere coincidence has been mostly rejected by the scientific community.

I also researched the 'death clinics' she had mentioned. From what I could find, just under a thousand people committed suicide using Switzerland's assisted suicide services in 2017, though there was a note that more than 100,000 were on the "membership list" for the future. A search for instances in the Netherlands confirmed similar numbers. A Dutch euthanasia law from 2002 has allowed Dutch doctors to assist more than 50,000 people in their deaths. A strange side note from the view of souls, but relevant, considering how most Christians view suicide as a way *not* to get into Heaven.

Then I discovered physician-assisted suicide was even legal in a handful of states in the United States. (Oh, the things learned along the way. You can pull that little knowledge nugget out at your next dinner party... perhaps to start a conversation about what *not* to talk about at a dinner party.)

But before I had enough time to fully digest everything Dr. Holzinger had said, it was time for my second interview of the day. This time, not from someone across the map, but just across the snow-covered corn fields.

It is us who direct fate

The Humanist

AFTER READING ABOUT Audrey Kingstrom, I was worried she wouldn't be interested in being interviewed. A humanist activist and educator, I came across her information during a strange internet tangent.

Searching for a way to contact a famed medium and author, I came across an article debunking her and her abilities as a medium. The debunking article was written by a member of the Center for Inquiry (CFI). I learned more about CFI and saw they had a Speakers Bureau available. Selecting Minnesota as the location, it narrowed the contacts down to just six individuals. I selected a woman I thought had a background that might match up with a soul search and emailed her. She never emailed back, making her the first "declined to be interviewed" on my list by default. But in her profile, it said she was also a member of the American Humanist Association. Upon reading about that organization, it, too, linked to local chapters. Clicking on Minnesota brought up the Humanists of Minnesota, a group based in Minneapolis. There was Audrey's contact information, along with another website to read.

The web of information led me to email addresses for both the medium as well as Audrey Kingstrom. The medium declined to be named within this book, while Audrey agreed—opposite of what I'd expected.

Audrey and I met through video chat rather than in person because of the extreme winter taking place outside. From where she was seated, I could see that her view out the window mirrored mine: whiteout conditions. Her husband was briefly on the screen, assisting with the technical aspects of getting the laptop microphone and camera up and running. I smiled, seeing they were both wearing warm, fleece vests that matched in color.

I began our conversation with my usual overview of the book. I explained my aim was to interview people from several walks of life regarding the evidence, if any, of a human soul.

"Why?" Audrey asked.

So far in my interviews, Audrey was the first to ask me *why*.

Ah, *why*. The question that had cursed me my entire life. I always wanted to know why. And if I had been on the other side of my interview requests, *why* would have been the first thing I asked. But so far, no others had.

"Beyond my curiosity," I told the unfamiliar face on the other side of the laptop screen, "I have interest in psychology and consciousness and I was taken to a past life regression where I saw other lives. But I don't know that I believe in other lives. So, I'm collecting interviews to see if I can find a commonality among opinions."

Audrey's blue eyes gleamed. Her hair was short and light in color. "So this is a personal search?"

I nodded, feeling almost ashamed to admit that this was, indeed, a personal quest that I hoped would also help others. Once we'd clarified our *why*, I dove into the questions. "First," I said, officially starting the interview. "How would you describe your professional role?"

"I am a Humanist Celebrant, and educator and a writer," she stated. "I was raised in rural Minnesota by a conservative farm family—traditional Lutheran, mainstream. During college, I joined an evangelical group and got very involved. This was at the time of the Vietnam War and near the end of the Civil Rights Movement—I was very influenced by the times," she added. "Even then, I was driven by philosophical questions, so eventually I started having doubts about God's goodness but kept them to myself. I had been a social work major, so after college I started working at a Christian Boys and Girls Club serving mostly low-income children," she said. "I really struggled then with so many questions about why God would let such inequities occur. Reconnecting with my Lutheran heritage, I started seminary in the late 1970s in Minneapolis. But studying theology and history only produced more questions and doubts about my faith. A pastor mentor suggested a non-denominational seminary in New York City. So off I went in the early 1980s during a time of religious diversity, the feminist movement, and liberation theology..."

I was writing and nodding, already fascinated with the story. I had contacted Audrey for a humanist and, I assumed, atheist viewpoint, and she was talking about seminary.

"It took six years to get a degree. I was working part-time and going to school. Doubts had started creeping up even before seminary—I guess you could call it *torment*. I had been very religious all my life. But by the time I finished my Master of Divinity degree, I didn't believe in God anymore and I wanted no part of religion."

"You finished the degree?" I blurted. "Sorry, but I wasn't expecting that."

"Yes," Audrey said. "I completed seminary, but later went on to receive a second master's degree in education and then taught high school social studies. I still wanted to help the world," she explained. "But when I no longer believed in God,

I had to figure out a better way to make a difference. I also became involved in political activism—which is how I met my husband. We stayed on the East Coast for several years, but when we had our second child, it was too difficult to continue teaching. Shortly thereafter, I moved my family to Minneapolis and we became involved with the Unitarian Universalists."

"I have not heard of that group," I confessed.

"It's a mixed group of liberal Christians, pagans, naturalists, humanists—people who are spiritual, but not religious."

I nodded, having heard that definition many times from my peers, and having used it to describe myself.

Audrey continued, "It is a little churchy for some. It was to me at first. The format may trigger some, but my husband and I wanted to get involved in a community for our family. By the early 2000s, atheism and secular humanism were gaining more attention nationally. National secular leaders were encouraging people to become humanist "celebrants" to better meet the needs of the growing secular demographic. So I decided to get endorsed as a Humanist Celebrant and involve myself with the local secular humanist group."

"So, in general, would you say humanists or universalists believe in a soul?" I asked.

"Secular humanists, I would say, would not. But religious humanists might. The naturalists—they believe in only what is of this earth. Nothing outside of this world; only what they can touch and feel. For all of us, things must be very evidence-based. Verifiable."

"Interesting. So having been on both sides of this, why do you think people hold such strong religious beliefs?"

Audrey looked at her ceiling. Behind her was an ornate, stained-glass, hanging light over a dining table. "We are products of how we are raised. But it's also more than that. I was raised a Lutheran on a farm. My husband was raised just outside of New York City, also Lutheran. But he decided by about junior high that he couldn't believe any of it. Me, on the other hand, I was diligent in my Lutheran confirmation process. I was an eighth-grade anomaly, a philosophical type. I took it all very seriously."

I couldn't help but think back to myself at that age. I had a mountain of creative writing and a case of cassette tapes filled with music I wrote, kept since junior high. Perhaps Audrey and I were not that different.

"I think it's also about the God of the gaps."

I looked up from my notepad. "God of the gaps?"

"It's a phrase common with atheists. It's the idea that God was the explanation for the unexplainable. Before we had modern medicine, people didn't know how to explain what was happening when people were ill. They said people were possessed by the devil. God was the explanation in our gaps. But the more knowledge increased, the less God was needed to fill the gaps."

I underlined the phrase. I discovered that while some agreed with Audrey's definition, theologians had turned it around, saying the gaps in science were in fact *proof* of God.

"The sun is going to rise, gravity will pull, snow will fall," Audrey continued. "We will be affected by the elements, but it doesn't have to be a higher being in control."

"So if no God, then what do you think happens after we die?"

Audrey did a small shrug and said, "Compost."

I couldn't help but chuckle. "Compost?"

"We didn't exist in this exact formulation of chemicals before we were born and nothing is ever really destroyed... so that material or energy will still exist after we die, but not in this form or this life."

I noticed the similarities in some of the interviews thus far. Before I started my soul interviews, I didn't know so many people believed we could be reduced to sheer energy particles.

Audrey continued, "When I die, I will exist only in the memories of others. Human culture sets us apart from other animals. We know musicians, writers, artists and leaders of the past. They live on in memory. And I do not find this depressing. We have the opportunity to live. To make contributions. To experience the wonderful sensations of life on this planet. I am part of something greater than myself. In fact, through science, I'm able to experience even more. Looking up at the night's sky suddenly becomes a view of eternity after learning about science and history. There is so much there. It's not sad or depressing. It's exciting."

"So you are not afraid to die?" I asked.

"I'm not afraid of death," she stated clearly. "Of course, most people don't want a painful or horrible death, but I believe in living well and dying well. And it's not that I won't be sad," she said with a far-off look. "For me, it's the people in my life and being a citizen of the world and the wellbeing of the planet that I'll be sad about. I won't get to see how those stories end. Communities and change and politics and progress—it will all go on. It will be like not getting to watch the end of a movie," she concluded.

I enjoyed hearing her speak. She was motivational and realistic at the same time. "My final question," I said after an hour of conversation, "Is if you believe that there are any unseen forces in the universe that can lead people with signs?"

She shook her head. "Nope. There's no force or energy that's directing things. Except for us. Political activists, humanists... we have human agency. We create the world we want to live in. There's no guarantee that the arc of history is long and actually leads to justice. In our own human agency, we can figure out how to fix things that are broken; how to help. Humanists can help people understand that it's *us* who direct the fate of the world. That's not to say we have control over the natural world, but we as humans have evolved to be able to accumulate knowledge, pass it on, and act intentionally to change the world. We have more to give in this world. We should all be giving."

After more chatting back and forth, Audrey and I said good-bye. But the palpable love for the human experience lasted for days. I wondered if a person could be a humanist and still believe in reincarnation. I wondered if I was technically a humanist. I wondered if that could be an answer for my agnostic husband.

And I wondered if I had ever fully thought about this being the one and only chance we had for experiences. I'd spent the past three years pondering living a revolving door of lives. And before that, I mostly believed that after this life, I would move on to a heaven scenario. But was that to escape the daunting reality that I was in my (late) thirties and had only achieved a handful of my life goals? If this was my one and only... I had a lot of work to do.

As I was scrolling through my online groups one evening, I came across a snip of psychological information that prompted a screenshot. It was the word *Pronoia*. Often defined as the opposite of paranoia, it was a word that offered me a new perspective. A person with pronoia would feel like the world around them, people with them, or the universe in general was always on their side, pushing them into good things. I had a strong understanding of paranoia, having several friends who regularly said things like, "It's like the whole world is against me!" But would a person who shouted, "It's like the whole world and universe is with me!" be viewed differently? Would that be a bad thing?

(Oh... per the internet, it would be a bad thing. It's a form of psychological delusion.)

In the year I was born, the word was coined by Dr. Fred H. Goldner in an academic journal entitled *Social Problems*. Dr. Goldner explained:

> *Pronoia is the positive counterpart of paranoia. It is the delusion that others think well of one. Actions and the products of one's efforts are thought to be well received and praised by others. Mere acquaintances are thought to be close friends; politeness and the exchange of pleasantries are taken as expressions of deep attachment and the promise of future support.*

Okay... would the law of attraction fall into this definition? Or believing in signs? I guess what I'm getting at is, would this be a fortunate or unfortunate trait that one might possess?

Asking for a friend.

I've tasted death enough to know I don't need to worry about it

The Medical Mystery

W ITH THOUGHTS OF our one and only shot at life per-
colating from Audrey's humanist point of view, I contacted a woman I had known in elementary school while living
in Wisconsin. She and I had been friends way back in sixth
grade (before the 1996 cold snap everyone kept referencing). I
linked up with her and sent her a message. She was on my
potential list because she had been in a terrible car accident
and nearly died, becoming a vocal advocate for the power of
prayer after her recovery. I sent her a message and asked if she
would be willing to speak about the incident and how it
affected her beliefs. She agreed, but wasn't available at the time.

The near-death aspect reminded me of an article I had written a year back, interviewing a phenomenal woman who had
lived through not one, but three near-death experiences. Her
name was Cecilia Baldwin, and she called herself *The Medical
Mystery Girl*.

Shortly after her fifteenth birthday, Cecilia Baldwin inexplicably began losing energy, strength and coordination. Too
tired to realize what was going on, in less than two months she
had inexplicably become a quadriplegic. With muscles seized
and lifeless, she was left only with the ability to blink her eyes,
barely move her lips and mercifully wiggle one finger. Her lung
capacity had been reduced to ten percent. She was in kidney

failure and severe liver distress. She was told to prepare for cardiac arrest. In the Intensive Care Unit, with reduced lung capacity, no peripheral nerve activity and continued multiple-organ failure, doctors were able to save her life, even though no one consulted was able to diagnose the cause. No one had a clue what had caused any of the ailments or symptoms. No one had answers.

Cecilia, now in her thirties, continues to battle an illness (or illnesses) that remains unseen and undiagnosed. She has been seen by doctors on two continents and countless specialists, often with the admission they're uncertain they have even identified all the symptoms, let alone what caused many of her internal systems to suddenly stop working as a teen. As she had spent so much time in hospitals fighting for her life, I was curious what Cecilia thought about all this soul stuff.

"I was raised in what I thought of as a typical, Christian family," she began. "Church on Sunday, youth groups on the weekend. When I got sick, my faith roots only got stronger... deeper," she told me. Housebound, as she can only sit up in her wheelchair for minutes at a time, Cecilia communicated with me through her computer.

"I am patiently typing this out on my couch in the sunroom, where there are curtains to limit the light when I need to. My legs are outstretched, a board sitting on top of two pillows across my 'lap' to hold the weight of the keyboard and support my arms. On a table next to me is an extra-large computer screen, so I can zoom in as my eyes fatigue (as all of my muscles were affected). You will always find my white, standard poodle, service dog, Camelot, valiantly by my side."

"I really appreciate you taking the time to talk to me. It means a lot. I'm sorry if it's terribly uncomfortable," I told the lovely young woman eight states over.

"I live reclined, with my legs propped up and my back and head fully supported—at best a forty-five degree angle. As I have a phobic-like tendency to avoid staying in bed all day, my life is a delicate balance from one position to another... In short, I welcome the distraction."

"Okay then," I told her. "I'll just jump right in with my questions. Do your Christian beliefs include the idea that humans have a soul outside of their physical being?"

"Yes," she stated. "I believe the soul is separate from the body; it's not something that is created from the mind, or our human persona that we could modify. I believe it's our entity, our quintessential essence that isn't as fickle or reactionary as what we often define our *metaphorical* heart. Nor is it something that can be crafted, changed or redirected like the mind."

"That's a beautiful explanation," I opined. "Why do you believe that?"

Cecilia explained, "When I became a neurologically-defined quadriplegic, there was no accident, cause or reason anyone could find. And the disease that caused it left a mess in its wake by leaving no identifying features. Because of that, doctors either respect the ghostly disease itself or, feeling bested, blame the patient—me—as being the cause. I have had my share of years of being blamed as the cause—being told I was psychotic and that it was all a play for attention. For a few years, the pressure was intense and the doctors' zeal to prove it unremitting."

"I'm sorry, I can't imagine being accused of such a thing."

"Yes, so if my soul was defined by mind, or subject to that ability to morph and change, my essence would not be that of the same person as I was pre-sickness. As it is, my core hasn't changed. In fact, it's my soul that has preserved me and kept me going despite the numerous, continuous obstacles."

"You have such a unique perspective, Cecilia. Thank you so much for sharing. I have to ask—in your time dealing with this disease, did you have any near-death experiences?" I asked.

"I've had several near-death experiences. I suppose it's bragging rights no one seeks in life. All of mine have been due to my illness. In an odd way, by having nearly died multiple times, I've learned there is a repetitive quality to it, as crazy as that sounds. You can never adjust to it. For me, each time, I feared going... dying... before it was my time. In my case, I didn't (and don't), want to die without a diagnosis, without having the peace of knowing what has caused so much upheaval in my body, and what has so changed not only the course of my life, but also my family's. Yet, the problem with near-death is that it shows you how powerless, how out of control you are. It's not exactly surrendering, but it's accepting that life and death have a force so much bigger than your own."

"Did the experiences affect you spiritually, physically or mentally?"

Cecilia grew solemn. "I'm not a fatalist," she stated, full of resolve. "I was raised to believe that we were all born with a divine purpose, and our timing is by God's will. I want to believe this, but I have seen too many amazing people lose their own battles to claim any understanding that people live based on their goodness, actions or potential. To reconcile this paradox, I simply believe that life—both life's whims and God's omniscience—is much bigger than I am humbly able to comprehend. I have come to accept that for some reason, some of us are around for longer on this Earth than others. But that being said, these experiences have changed me in unexpected ways. The first time I nearly died, it made me feel blessed. The second time, I grew leery. And then after that, it made me harder on the inside. I don't believe I was lucky or spared for some master plan. I just know I am still here and, because of that, I'm going to live as fully as possible."

"That's good advice for any of us," I agreed. "Would you mind sharing any of your experiences?"

"I will share one," she agreed. "The first was in 2002, when my unknown illness was at an acute stage with multiple organ failures, in addition to complete paralysis. I was in Buenos Aires, Argentina—where we lived at that time—being treated at an excellent hospital in an Intensive Care Unit. At my last testing, my lung capacity had been measured at below ten percent. The typical medical standard, when your health is that precarious, means you are intubated somewhere around thirty percent lung capacity. However, my doctor made the decision, with my mother's knowledge, to let my body crash, going into complete respiratory failure before beginning resuscitation, including intubation."

"Oh," I replied. "Why?"

"The reason he chose to do this was that a few hours before, he had started me on a medicine that he hoped would reverse the decline. His belief, which most agree with, was that if I were intubated, my brain would not remember how to move my lungs and I would never be taken off. He chose to give me every opportunity of letting the medication win before making a life-long change. And I am so grateful for his decision," she opined. "Fortunately, in the wee hours of the morning, I did begin to improve and the crash cart at the foot of my bed was never used."

"But before the morning? Was that the night of your near-death experience?"

"It's funny," Cecilia replied, "I did have an out-of-body experience with my first near-death... yet to this day, I don't like to talk about it."

I felt sheepish. "I'm sorry to have asked."

"What I can share was that I had a supernatural peace that night, when I knew something was wrong, but was not aware of the critical nature—and I *had* gone critical. My memories from late that night were all as viewed from above, like my eyes were looking down at the room. Looking down from above and seeing my mother's body slumped against the side of my hospital bed, gripping my hand, praying. I could hear her from above—her whispering throughout the night that I could not leave her. I also knew I was not alone up there as I watched the scene below," she paused. "The next morning, what I shared was that of seeing a dark-like fog move up my body, stopping at my chest. The darkness wasn't scary or ominous; it just was."

"Interesting..." I didn't know what to say, though her account was so similar to the others in the BBC documentary I'd watched. I took a breath and asked my next question. "Are you afraid of death?" I asked timidly.

"I'm not afraid of dying or what comes next. I have complete peace about the afterlife. But I am afraid of dying too soon—before I have answers for myself and my family."

"And what do you believe happens to a soul after the body dies? And did that change at all before and after your health issues were discovered?"

Cecilia answered, "As a Christian, I was raised to believe that there is an afterlife—Heaven with God, or Hell without God. While I do still believe in Heaven and Hell, I think any childish notions or detailed visions of what that looks like have all vanished. I have no finite views of what it will look like or what it entails. In some ways, I have tasted death enough to know that I don't need to worry about it. I choose to focus on being alive now; the rest will take care of itself whenever it arrives."

"That's a wonderful sentiment. And what are your thoughts on reincarnation?"

Cecilia did not pause before replying, "I don't believe it's impossible. I don't believe I have lived before... and part of me hopes not, as my soul feels battle-tested enough as is."

"How about the belief that there are forces able to guide people with signs or signals?"

She surprised me by simply answering, "Yes."

"How so?" I inquired.

"I don't believe in coincidences," she said. "When I open my eyes to all the little blessings around, I find it impossible *not* to find signs or signals. Most of them are so unexpected, one might not credit it."

"I think I agree," I told her. "I have seen signs everywhere as far back as I can remember. Maybe it's a physical or mental thing—to see synchronicity? But I seem fine-tuned for it."

"Me too," she agreed.

"Do you have any examples that come to mind?"

"Oh yes! One took place the summer before my freshman year of high school, before I became ill. I came across a fiction book, whose name I can't recall, that had a character who was a Navy SEAL. I had never heard of that Special Forces group before that time. I wasn't a particular armed forces enthusiast, but I was so intrigued I started to do research. Then, I did *a lot* of research. My family lived overseas at the time, so within the expat community, I knew some retired servicemen, and I began peppering them with questions. By the end of my freshman year of high school, I was a Navy SEAL devotee, knowing everything about the training process, mentality, drive, colorful language, et cetera."

"Colorful language?" I chuckled. "Like what?"

Cecilia declined to say, but continued her story. "Well, no

one could have imagined that before my sophomore year of high school even started, I would become a quadriplegic with little lung capacity. HOOYAH! Three years later after that, all of that Navy SEAL knowledge was put into full force, literally saving my life. I was admitted to a physical therapy rehabilitation center—one of the best in the world—but at the time my diagnosis status was considered psychosomatic, and my doctors were determined to prove once and for all that I was acting, which was in complete disregard that my psychiatric evaluation proved I was sane."

"My gosh, that's terrible. I'm sorry..."

"The doctors decided to do pool therapy, and told the physical therapist, without giving me any warning or instruction, to let me be face down in the pool—no floatie or human around. It was the longest couple of minutes of my life. I couldn't feel my therapist, and after a couple of attempts, confirmed I didn't have the neck strength to roll my head to lift my mouth out of the water. But, because of my Navy SEAL fanaticism, I knew to exhale—not hold my breath or intake! And I knew not to panic. In fact, I kept telling myself SEALs do this all the time, so it was nothing special. In that way, I had company in my head. The doctors didn't know then that I had severely diminished lung capacity, so even the short length of time was too much for me. By the time the pool session ended, I honestly thought I had died. I lost consciousness, only coming back to the pounding on my back and head to shake all the water out of my chest, ears and every other cavity in me."

I couldn't stop shaking my head. It sounded like a sci-fi movie with cruel, inhumane testing.

"I reflected later on," Cecilia concluded, "at how cosmic the timing was that I happened to have been a studious SEAL fan.

After all, if I had read a book with an Army Ranger, it would have served me no good in that situation... I may have died."

Hooyah...

After my interview with Cecilia, I spent a lot of time thinking about fate and destiny. I had never been one to believe in fate, though I probably should have, based on how my life had panned out. The way I found my "mother of the heart," Vicki, seemed like more than a coincidence.

In 2005, I began working at a senior center. I was driving home to my parents' house every weekend, severely missing being part of a family. I was lonely and lacked purpose. I was depressed. I had told several people I was thinking about moving back home because it was so difficult to have no close-by support system. Then, on a particular casual Friday, I wore my lime green Converse shoes to work. (Hey, I was in my twenties.) I was at my desk, typing away, when out in the hall I heard someone say, "Now those are some bright shoes!"

I looked up, assuming they were at my office door looking in, but no one was there. Out in the hall, I heard a woman cheerfully reply, "That they are! Lime green is my favorite color."

I got up and went to look into the hallway. Coming toward me was a woman who literally shined with cheery zest.

"I just have to stop you," I said, sticking my foot out into the hall. "Because I don't often meet others with a love of lime green footwear."

"Look at that!" she cried, touching toe to toe with my matching shoes. We looked into each other's eyes and smiled.

And that, as they say, was that.

Though I'm young enough to be her daughter (in fact, she has a daughter just one year older than me), we became fast friends. We had an eerily long list of things in common, including the fact that I missed my family and she missed hers, her daughter living across the country. I started having dinner with Vicki and her husband at least once a week. I became friends with her friends. She introduced me to everyone in town—including the mayor. Vicki's husband, Bruce, was a city councilman. And when he was up for re-election, he asked me to work on his campaign, beginning my freelance marketing and writing career. Vicki and Bruce supported me through dates and boyfriends, breakups and moves, a wedding and babies. Fourteen years later, they were still a part of my daily life.

I bring this up because they are who led me to meet Kitty Karn. And Kitty was my next interview.

Always a soul.
Not always a body.

The Kundalini Yoga Musician

I N FEBRUARY, JUST before my birthday, I set up an interview with Vicki's sister, Kitty Karn. Kitty held the same
magnetism as Vicki—a beautiful family trait, it seemed. But
while Vicki's robust, overt love of the simple joys in life like
good friends, good conversation and good books seemed to
cause her to glow, Kitty's joyful nature seemed to be gleaned
from her love of music, yoga and animals.

Kitty Karn, MA is an Associate Professor of Musical The-
atre and Voice at a state university. She also practices Kundalini
yoga (which again I must admit, I had never heard mentioned
before my journey).

I sat down to interview Kitty, computer-to-computer, on a
Friday. My three-year-old son was playing on the tablet in the
other room—an educational app he didn't realize was part of
the reason he could already sight-read a couple words. He was
a factor in setting up the interview with a music professor.

At age three, he had already reminded me so much about
how music shaped me. Whenever he heard a particularly moving song, he started to cry. Perhaps strange, but I could relate.
I went through most of my life with tears prickling my eyes or
hairs standing on end when I was surrounded by full, passion-
ate music.

During my school life, I played three instruments, participated in several school bands, two choirs and lettered in high school music. I didn't know my strong link to music was something that could be passed down to my children. Yet at three, my son has all the passion and pitch and fervor. Music moves him. Whether spiritual, emotional or some chemical imbalance of the brain thanks to my genes, I wasn't sure. But because of the link we have to music and a spiritual feeling, Kitty was a perfect candidate for my next conversation.

Kitty was seated in her university office when we connected. After greeting one another and getting our cameras adjusted, I gave her the overview of the book. She adjusted her trendy glasses, causing me to smile at her jazzy scarf and dangling pearl earrings. She sparkled inside and out.

"So I'm just going to jump right in," I stated. "Can you explain to me what Kundalini yoga is and what led you to it?"

Her smile beamed. "Well, I'm a child of the sixties," she explained with a familiar laugh. "I grew up in small-town Minnesota in a Catholic family, as you know. And by the eighties, I was a voice student in Texas. By the nineties, I had started practicing yoga, where they specifically '*warned*' us never to practice Kundalini," she said, complete with air quotes and a touch of sarcasm.

I accidentally made a face. It sounded ominous.

Kitty continued, "Later, I was told Kundalini was the very thing that could change my energies and improve my voice through chakras. I began practicing and I could not believe my transformation!" She shook her head in continued disbelief. "I was hooked! As it turned out, there was a class that was mere blocks from my house. I began going four times a week. There was a misconception at that time that it was connected with drugs and people 'flipping out,'" she said, again using air quotes. "But in reality, the guy who brought Kundalini into the states was trying to get people *off* of drugs by using a natural high instead. But if a person practiced it while they were high, it would take them higher and higher and become dangerous because it would work too fast on the nervous system. But that's not a concern for me. So, for me and many others, it's just the boost that is needed."

I was nodding. "So out of curiosity, which do you find more spiritual—Kundalini yoga or music?"

Kitty leaned back and looked up for a moment. "That is a tough question... I guess I would say that they are inextricably linked." She intertwined her fingers in front of her laptop camera. "I'm basing this on the science of mantra and chanting. Chanting opens channels to the most authentic *you*. The most *you* you can be... really show your soul as beautifully and authentically as possible. So I really couldn't separate them. Together, they are an art form."

"What a wonderful explanation," I opined. "So as a form of art, do you think anyone could do this art form? Benefit from it?"

"Yes," she answered easily. "Anyone could do this. Singing on its own is *very* healing and it can link us to community and fight depression. It's an outlet to uplift us."

"That's beautiful and I fully agree. I have always felt a connection to music," I shared. "So you mentioned 'showing your soul.' I assume this means you believe humans have a soul?"

"Oh, yes," Kitty agreed. "We are always a soul, not always a body," she stated with vim. "In my own personal soul journey, I formed my inner belief that the soul is eternal. It may go to a place where there's no physical matter, but it can still communicate. I also believe in soul groups," she added with a smile.

Soul groups were a concept I had first heard about a few

years prior while I was writing my debut novel. As Kitty had read the book (and was even mentioned in it), I could tell she was poking me for a response.

Kitty continued with a smirk, "You can call it twin flames or soul groups, but I truly believe there is a small group of people connected throughout the journey. I'm sure you know that Vicki is in your soul group."

"She is?" I blurted, darting my face up from my notepad.

Kitty nodded. "I believe she is."

Now I was smiling. What a thought. Had I been drawn to Vicki by some soulmate-ish force? I didn't know the answer. But I was open to pondering it.

Kitty tilted her head, causing her pearl earrings to shimmer as she continued, "I also think some of these beings in the group could be somewhere else, as in not on Earth, maybe in an ethereal place. And where the group resides, a piece of your own soul resides. Keeping the group together..." she trailed off and was quiet for a moment. "The more I've sat with that thought, the more I feel like it's true. Because I think there are certain people in our life that we meet, but we already *know* their essence. Sometimes it can even be recognized within their eyes. And we gravitate toward one another."

"Do you feel like you've found members of your soul group?"

"I do," she replied.

"Does that make you feel more secure? Less afraid of death?"

"I am not afraid of death," she said with a head shake. "I just took a fascinating class, a level-two yoga course called *Life Cycles and Lifestyles*. There were a few days spent on the topic of death. Of that group, only one of eleven was afraid of dying."

I chimed in, "Of all those I've interviewed so far, not one

person has told me they were afraid of dying. That surprises me." I looked to my next question. "And do you believe in reincarnation?"

"I haven't spent too much time thinking about it, but I do think I've seen bits and pieces of lives through past life regressions. I've had many people tell me incredible stories of other lives."

It was at this point that my son wandered into my home office to tell me the tablet needed to be plugged in. I was relieved Kitty was familiar enough with my family to take the intrusion as an adorable side perk of the interview. She called to him by name and waved to him through the laptop from her university in Illinois. His little face looked like the television had just started talking to him! He ran away, and I helped him get settled again—away from the spooky computer that knew his name.

After apologizing, I moved on to the next question about signs. "Do you believe there are signs sent to lead us in a certain direction," I asked.

"I do. I believe because it has happened to me. You see, when I was in my first year of teaching, I had an astrological reading that said in the spring I would meet my person—the love of my life. I sort of believed it, but sort of didn't. I was lonely, so—doing what Kitty does best—I got into a serious relationship," she said with a self-directed eye roll. "Then I was asked to be on a search committee for a new jazz pianist. I was handed a plain manila folder with just a name on it... and I *just knew*. I felt like I knew his essence. It was so powerful, I felt like I might faint. This would be my Michael. Well, since I was already in a relationship, it took three years before I got together with Michael, but we are together now. And he really is the love of my life."

"That's so beautiful," I couldn't help but add.

Kitty smiled. "I did have one other experience I wanted to be sure I mentioned."

"Okay," I said. "Please do."

"It was a significant experience. I had a cat named Sebastian," she began. "He came into my life at a really dark time. He was the only being who moved with me from Illinois to Texas and back to Illinois. Then, three years ago, Sebastian died."

"I'm sorry," I sympathized, seeing how difficult it was for her to talk about him.

She nodded and continued. "I was holding him right next to my heart when he died," she said with tears starting to form in her glittering eyes. "I don't know how else to explain it, but when Sebastian died, I felt his soul move through me."

"Really..." I was engrossed in the story and had stopped writing to watch Kitty's explanation.

"It was as close to spiritual ecstasy as I've ever experienced. It was the most profound feeling of bliss I've ever known. I felt his soul pass through my heart, the center of my neck and out through the top of my head." She motioned with her hand and I could picture exactly what she was saying.

"That is astounding. I've never heard of that happening."

Kitty dropped her hand down to point. "And you know, I didn't think of it at the time, but I learned at a class that if you've really let go of a lot of karma and were a truly loving and beautiful soul, when you die—if your lives lined up and you cleared your karma—you leave a body from the crown chakra and make it through..." She paused, motioning above her head. "Sebastian was so light. He helped me so much. If anyone could make it through, it would be him. And I'm thankful he was able to share that with me."

After my interview with Kitty, I concentrated on how I'd viewed my four deaths in my four regressions. Two, I was unsure about. But in the other two, I did recall leaving the body from the chest and stomach area.

A chakra guide said the chest was the Heart Chakra, which somehow made sense, since I think I had viewed the chest as the location the soul left in my first past life vision of Jean the French Canadian, the loving husband and father. The stomach was called the Solar Chakra, often associated with sunshine and positivity, which again, was engrossing, as that was the location associated with Sweat Bea the humanitarian living in the 1960s.

Where the soul left the body was something I made note to pay special attention to when I did my next past life regression.

Those who have left us

W HEN I CAN'T sleep for any reason, I compose things in my mind. Not music, but words. I write up entire emails to people, essays, articles and chapters, all dictated by that secret inner voice in my head. Unfortunately, they never seem to flow once I'm awake to write. It's just what I do when I can't sleep.

One night, I started thinking about an important person in my life who had died. I don't know why his face was suddenly hung like posters around the halls of my thoughts, but there he was. His name was Steven. I composed an entire short essay in my mind, imagining sending it to his relatives. His family had never known how special he was to me... and maybe vice versa.

You see, after I left a four-year-long relationship and moved to a new town, I worked with Steven at a music store selling guitars. It was a job unlike any I had ever had before. Previous to my musical instrument sales, I'd been the assistant manager of a community food shelf while attending college (cliché do-gooder, as my ex had called me). Because of the job at the music store, I ended up meeting a joyful, ramshackle group of local musicians who completely took me into their lives and helped me adjust to my new city. They took me along to gigs, usually in the backseat crammed next to several leather instrument cases. They introduced me to all types of peculiar and kind people. And at work, we had many hours together, pacing the floors, waiting for customers. (There wasn't a line out the door for clarinet reeds and guitar floor stands, even before Amazon.)

Steven seemed to have a crush on me back then—I, fresh out of college, and him, a year younger. But he also seemed to have a crush on all the girls working at the music store, so I didn't linger on the thought too much. He and I had many deep talks, as young people getting to be friends often do, and I encouraged him to go to school for music. He was a brilliant and talented guitarist. I spent hours listening to him play, all the while with him cracking lewd jokes to make me laugh.

Months later, I visited Steven in his new college town and a group of us hit the local bars. By the end of the night, he was not well enough to be left alone so I took a taxi with him to his apartment. (Yes, this pre-dated Uber.) I practically had to carry him up the stairs, which wasn't that difficult seeing as how I was about a foot taller than him. (A fact Steven often joked about, reminding me that everyone was the same height laying down.)

When I got to his bedroom, he crashed onto the bed. The taxi was waiting, so I had to go. He grabbed my hand and mumbled something about needing me. When I looked at his wall, I was shocked and humbled to see notes I'd written him taped up. Notes encouraging him to beat his mental demons and succeed. To choose joy. To pursue music. To ask for help. I'd written them over a year ago with no reply from him. And there they were... hanging next to his bed.

I'm sad to say I left him then. I had to get back to my own town and life. And after that point, our lives went opposite directions and we drifted apart. I don't think there were more than a few messages between the two of us for years. I tried to invite him to my wedding, but no one seemed to know his address all those years later. Then I tried to tell him I'd had a baby, but again my messages seemed to go unread.

And then, one day, I logged into Facebook and saw a number of messages on his wall with condolences.

Steven was dead.

And he and I were so far removed that if I hadn't been connected with him through social media, I wouldn't have even known. I didn't know any of the relatives posting the tragic news. I took his death pretty hard. Steven was wild and reckless and hilarious and talented, but always hurting, it seemed. I mourned his death deeply.

Before his death, he had popped back on social media after deleting his account. I quickly re-friended him and wrote, "Hey! You're alive!" on his wall. A few days later, he responded by writing on my wall, "Holy shit! I'm alive!" And now, each year on the same day, Facebook shows me that memory. Only now, it's eerie and sad. A message from the past.

The night after I narrated my special memories of Steven in my mind, my best friend (who also knew him) texted that she saw an obituary for a Steven with a similar last name, which made her also reminisce about him. I pointed out the strange timing, feeling a little like it was a clairvoyant moment for me. There was a belief out there that the more you tapped into your higher self, the more clairvoyant you became. This was a belief I'd pondered hard because right after I attended a past life regression, I texted a close friend I hadn't spoken to in months because I suddenly and randomly felt sure she was pregnant. When she didn't text back the next day, I wondered if I had been right. When I saw her name pop up on my caller ID, I answered by exclaiming, "You ARE pregnant?" And yes, she was.

Was I honing in on some type of skill? I didn't know. I

didn't even know if I believed in it. But no one in my friend group had mentioned Steven in years, so it felt odd that I obsessed about him the night before my best friend brought up his name.

After chatting about Steven, I was struck with the realization that I hadn't ever seen an obituary for him, or heard about a funeral.

I started a crazed digging for details. I searched local records, county records... I even went so far as to sign up for one of those questionable online sites that knows everything about everyone. But time and time again, nothing came up. Steven's death was noted nowhere that I could find.

I had a few hours of time where I was shaking, wondering if Steven had somehow faked his own death—which, trust me, wasn't something I went around accusing people of, but he was the kind of guy who might have considered it.

I reeled with questions. If he was alive, where was he? Did his family know? Was he waiting for someone to come looking for him? Was he out there playing guitar on a beach somewhere, just waiting?

My best friend assured me I was being ridiculous. And the cannonball in my stomach agreed. So, taking a cue from Steven, I did something pretty wild and reckless... I sent a message to his sister, whom I had never met, asking for a link to his obituary.

While I was waiting, I called my dad. As a genealogist, he had subscriptions that offered access to records I didn't have. I sent off my friend's name and waited for his reply.

It was only an hour later that my father wrote back. His email was simple, yet struck me like a pin to a full birthday balloon. Steven had no obituary, but records showed that he died in July 2014. He was buried a few towns over from my current residence, in a small countryside cemetery.

Relieved and saddened at the same time, I then received a reply from Steven's younger sister. She was sweet and didn't seem put-off at my rude questions. Instead, she was happy to hear that Steven was being remembered. I told her about adding Steven to my book and she linked me to an older sister. His older sister messaged me as well, her profile picture one of her and Steven standing together, happy smiles on their faces. She confirmed that he did not have an obituary, which was why I could never find it, and was also pleased to hear that Steven would live on, even if in a small way such as in this book. We had a lovely email chat ending with my promise to let her know when the book published.

So with Steven truly gone from this Earth, I rounded back through all I had learned so far. Was he up in some energy world, awaiting reunion with his loved ones before returning for another life on Earth? Had he turned back into molecules that were now growing into an apple? Was he just gone, except for living on in our memories?

I asked a couple of close friends, my husband included, if it was more or less comforting to think of deceased loved ones being in Heaven, as dispersed molecules or already reborn as someone else. So far, all have said Heaven—or at least some unknown place where our souls hover and wait before the next step in the process—brought them the most peace.

In the version of the energy world I viewed in my past life regressions, there were no physical things. But I still like to imagine Steven relaxed and chill, plucking at his guitar and smiling in that distant, contemplative way he always did.

When the several feet of snow melted, I vowed to visit Steven's grave.

Spiritual, mental & physical

THIRTY-FIVE DAYS LATER, it was April, and I was well enough to write again. Thinking I had figured out how to balance a million priorities, with impossibly high expectations and standards—mothering, working, freelance article deadlines, book interviews and writing—getting sick with influenza had hit me like a gunshot, sending everything shattering to the floor.

I balanced all of my plates tediously and precariously until I was so sick, I started to cry trying to put on a sweater, then slept for fourteen hours straight. I'd been dealing with so much stress and panic and scheduling that I broke down to Craig, admitting that I needed to take actual sick days during one of my busiest work weeks of the year.

I continued to work through every flu symptom you can imagine. And when I physically couldn't go to the office, I napped until I could work from home. I missed my daughter's school conference. For the first time in a decade, I missed a freelance deadline. Even worse, I left a woman sitting in a coffee shop waiting for me to interview her for this very book, without so much as a text, because I'd let my phone die while in a flu fog. I was in so deep, I checked out from the world more than I had in years. A week and two seasons of *Golden Girls* passed, and I got worse instead of better. When I called a nurse, she asked, "Have you been getting enough sleep? Eating nourishing foods? Avoiding stress?" It was almost chastising, but I felt it was warranted. I'd been running on fumes for at least seven months. All of my answers to her questions were no. And I realized things needed to change. I didn't understand why a relatively healthy woman in her thirties would be hit for more than a week with a virus the children had passed in a handful of days.

Because I couldn't get around working on an annual event, I ended up putting in a ten-and-a-half-hour workday, despite an Urgent Care visit for a lung x-ray, thanks to a newly-developed barking cough that everyone suspected was pneumonia. I was told I needed to rest or the cough could develop into something worse.

But even though I was letting life fall apart around me by resting, I didn't get better like a healthy person, even after the event stress was over. Even after sleeping and resting. I didn't bounce back. I was ill for seventeen days, with another two weeks of slow and steady recovery from massive post-viral fatigue. Not only did it keep me from writing, but it made me acutely aware that I'd spent so much time researching and working to better my mental and spiritual health, yet I had completely avoided dealing with the physical.

I happened to reschedule an interview for the same week I started a nutrition regimen meant to improve my overall physical health. Law of attraction at play? My interview was with the hypnotherapist who had led all four of my past life regressions—and she was a Nutritional Therapy Practitioner, as well as an International Association of Counselors and Therapists (IACT) Certified Hypnotherapist.

I was on day five of a restrictive keto-type diet and nutrition program when I met Aileen Abliss at a coffee shop in town.

Gratitude is our link to the spiritual world

The Past Life Regressionist

I ARRIVED A few minutes early, to have time to use my handy smartphone app to determine a drink that was both low in carbs and low in caffeine. (I was less than a week in and already driving Craig crazy scanning every barcode before consumption.)

I found a drink that would work, and ordered. It was then I noticed the sign that the coffee shop would be closing for the night in one hour. I wasn't sure that was long enough. So far, my interviews had been completely free-flowing and human-dependent—some running as short as twenty minutes and others running up to two hours.

After finding a seat next to giant bins of coffee beans that, frankly, smelled like the road to Heaven itself, I was getting my trusty yellow notepad ready as Aileen entered.

"Hello!" I greeted with a wave. "I want to apologize again for leaving you waiting the other day," I begged her pardon.

She smiled and hugged me... which in turn made me smile and feel forgiven. Such a simple act with such a powerful impact.

We made small talk about my new foray into a healthier lifestyle through eating habits. She mentioned that she has done counseling for Overeaters Anonymous. I made a self-deprecating comment about consuming an entire bag of chips during a movie, which prompted a look. I mumbled a reiteration of my newfound commitment to my physical health, and propelled the topic back to the spiritual world. I had so many questions for the woman who had helped launch my search.

"So I'm curious about your background," I told the petite, strawberry blonde woman in front of me. "Did you go to church as a child?"

"I actually didn't," she said—the first of my interviewees to say so. "As a young adult, I joined the Methodist Church, but I'm not so active now."

"What led you to the practice of hypnotherapy and past life regressions?"

"Well," she started with a sweet smile, "about twelve years ago, I read Ekhart Tolle's *A New Earth*."

I looked at the woman in front of me, shaking my head. "I literally just got a copy of *The Power of Now* by Tolle two days ago, but haven't started reading it yet."

"Oh!" she added with another smile. "Well, at around that time, I attended a Qigong class and the teacher asked if anyone was interested in learning more about past lives after the class..." Aileen continued her story, but I underlined Qigong. Once again, I needed to look it up. She said, "If you had asked me at that point if I believed in past lives, I probably would have said no. Yet I found myself searching for more information."

"I can certainly relate to that!" I added, reminded of my first hypnosis experience with her a few years prior.

She tucked her hair behind her ear and leaned in to the table. "The teacher gave me a reading list. As a mom of six kids, I was not a voracious reader..."

"Six!" I interrupted.

She chuckled. "Yes, and most weren't teens yet. But somehow, I flew through the books!"

I was mentally stuck on the six kids mention. Two were causing me to feel like I was only a few commitments short of toppling over. Aileen had her own business and six kids and still made time for me. She was amazing. And I felt even more gratitude toward her.

She continued her story, "The first book on the list led me to find self-hypnosis, thanks to a free ebook, and I began daily self-hypnosis. After a month of reading and practicing, I knew I wanted to become a past life regressionist. I attended a class in alignment with the Newton Institute."

"I'm not familiar with the Newton Institute," I admitted. "But I'm assuming it's linked to the Michael Newton you mentioned, along with Brian Weiss, in your classes?"

"Yes, right. They hold trainings about past life therapy and life between lives."

"Fascinating... So *now* do you think they are real past life experiences?"

"I think so," she replied. "Though it doesn't matter if they are or aren't because they are so powerful!"

I nodded in agreement. Powerful, indeed. "Do you think the experiences could just be messages from the subconscious?"

She tipped her head in thought. "It's all about the messages. I believe the subconscious is the gateway to our soul. Our soul is the gateway to the spiritual world or love and guidance."

I caught myself nodding again. "And what led you to believe in a soul? You seem sure."

"I believe we all have a soul or energy or light. I like to think of it as inside the body, even though I believe a part of the soul remains in the spiritual world."

"Remains there while we are here?" I clarified.

"Yes. A small portion is always in the spirit world—energy world, Heaven, whatever you'd like to call it. I used to call it 'the other side,' but during a hypnotherapy session, a spirit guide said, 'Why do you call it that? Don't call it that.'" She laughed. I did too. Strange thing to be reprimanded by a spirit. She continued her explanation, "There are life goals and soul goals and they may or may not coincide. We may not know the majority of our soul goals, but instead choose life goals because we have free choice. But there are always lessons for our soul."

Her words sounded familiar. Most of the online groups and books I had read about past lives echoed a similar theme. We were here for the lessons. To grow. But what a lofty end goal when we don't even know the name of the game. "Do you have any idea what your soul lessons are?" I asked.

She shook her head. "No, but even if we don't know the lesson or reason, we shouldn't stop trying to better ourselves or to learn or grow as a person."

I was nodding. "Do you believe we are able to choose our soul lesson? Or choose which life we want to live here on Earth?" I asked, thinking of Pooja, who seemed so sure that we do.

"I'm unsure," she answered. "I believe at the time of choosing what lessons we will be working on we know, but when we get here, the soul lessons may not be so evident. I have a hunch one of my soul lessons involves forgiveness," she stated. "Through Michael Newton's books, I learned about hierarchy and levels. I heard about younger souls choosing lives with more lessons because they had more lessons to learn. I remember that in one of his books, Michael Newton said the most advanced soul he'd ever met was a waitress at a roadside diner in the desert."

"Interesting," I mused. "I think Michael Newton has passed away now?" I said of the institute founder, remembering what I'd read that first ravenous night of reading.

"Yes, in 2016, I think."

"So what do you think about spirit guides?" I asked, steering our conversation to cover all of my burning questions.

"I think the guides are able to offer choices. An easy life with fewer lessons for tired souls or difficult lives with much to gain for others."

"Huh," I grunted, struck by the thought. "So by picking a more difficult life on Earth, you're *leveling up* after this lifetime?"

She smirked. "Something like that. But I believe the soul comes back when it decides to come back. It wants to come back. For the beauty. Based on what I've read, some souls don't want to come back right away and others cannot wait to. To hold a baby in their arms again. To run along the bluffs, soaking in nature and the outdoors. It's so amazing! We come for the experiences."

Her words made the hairs on my arm prickle. Her words were so similar to Pooja's (Hindu), and Audrey's (Humanist), and even Dr. Parrino's (Neurologist). I was finding a common thread in the story. Humans are here for the experiences. Perhaps some of us for more turns than others. "Don't you ever find that thought exhausting? Living again and again?" I asked.

She shook her head a little. "I *do* believe we want to be here. But I recall a woman from New York at a session with that perspective. She argued with her spirit guides, telling them, 'I really don't want to be here.' They assured her that she had chosen to be there. They told her she had lessons to learn and, although tough, she needed to keep going before she could rest and recuperate in the spirit world. Her spirit guides not only reminded her she had lessons to learn, but also much to contribute in the way of helping others. So I believe that with the guides there, anyone could be talked into coming back again." She ended with a petite shoulder shrug.

It was about that time I glanced up to see the staff at the coffee shop cleaning up and preparing to close. I informed Aileen they were closing and we made our way across the road to the food co-op. "So back to what you were saying," I began, resettled into the leather chair next to Aileen. "If you complete a soul mission, do you go to a different ascension level?"

Aileen made a face. "Newton said there were levels, but I don't know much about that topic. My kids always ask me things like that. Like, 'what about Jeffrey Dahmer, what if he already came back to Earth?' And I've done reading on the topic of karma and ascension levels, but I just don't know what I think. Once, I read that terrible, evil people's souls are re-scrambled—completely reconfigured and mixed into other energies so that the one specific soul can never again exist."

"What a thought..." I mumbled, trying to picture a soul energy scramble.

Aileen nodded. "A fascinating idea," she agreed.

"After death, do you believe the soul returns to the spirit world—I won't call it *the other side*," I restated with a smirk. "Have you seen what it looks like? In life-between-lives hypnotherapy?"

"It's not so difficult to reach the spirit world," she answered easily. "Meditation, expressive writing, hypnotherapy—there are many ways to experience it. Even gratitude links us to the spiritual world. There is mindfulness training... anyone can do this. We *are* love, and we come to Earth to experience contrast. We are fully supported as we devote ourselves to our divine life purpose. I believe we are powerful creators of our lives, but also that the life lessons have been somehow predetermined prior to our incarnation. It's just not that difficult to see for yourself... prayer, imagination, helping others—it can all help us get there."

"You mentioned prayer. Does that mean you are still religious?"

"Faith is so important in this life," she said. "Because it is so engrained in this life, I think Heaven is what people view when they see the spirit world. It's like that book, *Heaven is For Real.*"

"Yes, I've read it. But it's a completely religious view of an afterworld..." I said, remembering the Todd Burpo book in which he details his preschool-aged son's near-death visit to Heaven.

"Yes, but what if it's just the same?" she asked. "What if angels are spirit guides; God is the boss? What if religious people view that version because that's what would make them the most comfortable? And others of us see glowing orbs and bright lights because we don't need that heavenly representation to feel comfort?"

I was nodding, seeing her point; a point I had pondered on my own.

"We are likely greeted by the familiar as we make important transitions."

"Yes, that seems a common theme in many near-death stories as well. So how many lives have you seen yourself live before?"

"I have seen two full and two partial," she stated. "And, for me, viewing them opened up possibilities. I felt supported. More courageous. Like I no longer needed to play it small because I was no longer restricted by those limitations. Ask and receive. It's in the Bible and it's true. It's empowering and encouraging and I often just meditate to say thank you for it all."

I was inspired and floating by the time we said our goodbyes at the back of the co-op. She sent me with a list of potential people to contact for more information, including a psychic medium she had consulted twice. "Do you think she'll know I'm going to call before I call her?" I jokingly asked Aileen. Without so much as a blink, she replied, "It doesn't work like that."

If only bad jokes got you closer to the spirit world, I'd be set.

I drifted down the fragrant aisles of the co-op, the only shopper left before closing, finding my MCT oil, fresh ginger and coconut butter for the new keto recipes, and was on my way after nearly three hours with Aileen—a new record.

When I got home, Craig had already put the kids to bed. I grabbed my phone and called my cousin, Becky, who had been the one to talk me into my first past life regression. I talked and recapped with vigor about soul goals and spirit guides, about the psychic medium who believed she could talk to those in the spirit world, about how gratitude could link us.

We talked through theories and ideas, energized by all the revelations. We ended the call with a promise to do another past life regression together. The only problem being, there wasn't another event scheduled in the area.

I couldn't sleep again that night. Craig guessed it was all the fat and protein I was digesting; I guessed it was energy from the hunt. I felt renewed and ready to learn as much as

I could. I looked up the psychic Aileen had mentioned and sent out an email. Ask and receive. I also looked up the definition of Qigong. Roughly translated, it was a type of moving meditation. The images online made me realize I'd seen people performing it in movies, but never in real life. The first time I'd ever seen someone practicing Qigong was in a movie called *Dream a Little Dream* from 1989 (Corey and Corey in all their glory, *and* another 1980s movie to add to the spiritual movie list). I'd only been around eight years old when I'd first watched it with my older sister. The movie synopsis stated that an elderly dream researcher's consciousness got stuck in a teenager's body.

Rereading the description of a movie I'd watched several times as a child made me wonder how much information was stored and forgotten up there somewhere. For me, it also awarded another point to the "past lives are just messages from the subconscious" team.

When the Mötley Crüe movie, *The Dirt*, hit Netflix, Craig and I were quick to watch it. Not actual fans of the band, but always fans of music, we had no expectations. When the movie ended, I turned to recap with him. "What if they're higher souls?" I asked him, pulling out my phone to search for more details on the band members.

Eyebrow hiked to his forehead, he replied, "Yeaaah... I don't think so."

"Why not? If you were born with some painful spine disease, you think you'd choose that lifestyle? A rigorous, relentless, painful physical life like that?"

He was shaking his head and smirking, a face I saw often. "You are the only person I know who can make being a rockstar sound like a horrible life."

"Well it is!" I argued. "Sort of. You're just a slave to your art, a slave to your fans... I couldn't do it. Even without ankylosing spondylitis."

He rolled his eyes at me reading directly from my smartphone. We both knew there was no way I recalled the medical term for Mick Mars' disease.

"So if they are advanced souls, what does that even mean?" he gave in and asked.

I shrugged. "What if they chose that life because it had tough lessons to be learned, but they also wanted to live their fullest life; live for the experiences. We know so many people who make choices based on fear," I kept ranting, feet tucked under me on the couch.

"Including us," Craig added with a small head bob.

"Right, but those guys lived like they weren't afraid of anything. They went through almost every human experience, even when they had really big difficulties in life."

"God, that part when the kid dies..." he interjected, slapping a hand to his chest. "I can't deal with that anymore."

I was nodding. "Anyway, makes you think."

"Makes *you* think, yeah. Maybe next time we can find a movie that you don't relate to all this soul stuff."

I scoffed. "I mean, if *this* wasn't it..."

An important discomfort

The Atheist

A T THE BEGINNING of my journey, I sent emails out into the wide world seeking interviews from opposing camps—atheists and humanists as well as psychics and light-workers. Stephanie Zvan took five months to email me back. She said my email had been marked as read, but she had never seen it. I enjoyed how my interview requests seemed to volley back and forth at the perfect time to create balance. I was thrilled to have her included, and we set up a time to talk.

I found Stephanie through the Center for Inquiry's website. She was listed as a radio host and writer. Her radio show, "Atheists Talk," is broadcast in Minnesota. In addition, her fiction has been published in *Nature* and *Scientific American*.

At the time of our interview, Stephanie introduced herself as the Associate President of Minnesota Atheists. So I began with the most basic of questions for her. "What *is* an atheist?" I know that may seem obvious, but I've run across a variety of atheists with different beliefs and 'pain points,' so I was curious to know Stephanie's point of view.

Through the laptop, the woman with wavy hair and glasses began, "I would define atheism as a lack of belief in any gods," she stated easily. "Atheism calls into question the societal narratives of what happens after death. Some believe, like humanists, that when you're dead, you're dead."

"Oh, I interviewed Audrey Kingstrom from Humanists of Minnesota," I inserted.

"Oh, yes, I'm familiar," Stephanie said.

"Her exact word for what happens after death was *compost*," I recited.

Stephanie let out a small laugh. "I'm glad you're getting opinions from all sides."

I smiled and dove back in. "So when you were growing up, was that the belief you were taught? That nothing happened after death?" I asked her.

She shook her head and looked to the side. "I was raised by parents who were Methodists, I'd say on the strict end. They decided to raise us without religion and allowed us to decide as we grew up. None of my three siblings chose a religion, though I'm the only one who identifies strongly as an atheist. Along the way, I studied many religions and mythologies. I had a brief flirtation with paganism," she said with a small chuckle. "But I found that ritual makes me feel silly."

"So, living in Middle America where everyone around seems to be following the same general religious rules, did you ever feel left out? Or out of place?" I was curious to know.

"I suppose maybe," she agreed with some reluctance. "But I'd say more outraged than out of place. Take Confirmation as an example. In junior high, I was the one asking my peers *why*, at age thirteen, they were making a life-long decision. I mean, thirteen!" she emphasized.

It was my turn to chuckle. "I had those same thoughts and concerns, yet I was scooted along with the group," I admitted. "I was confirmed," I stated, fearing judgment.

But none came. Stephanie seemed more sympathetic than quick to judge.

I jumped in with the next question. "What exactly is Minnesota Atheists?"

Stephanie took a breath and then gave an articulate overview. "Minnesota Atheists is the largest and longest-lasting atheist group in Minnesota. It started as a regional group of the American Atheists decades ago. But then the state chapters closed. Today, the organization has three parts to our mission. First, to provide a social space where people can land when they leave religion. Second, to work to educate and publicize who we are and what we believe. Third, to be activists. Because nobody else is going to make the world we want. We are active political and community activists."

"What would be an example of something you advocate for?" I asked, intrigued by the group.

"There are a lot of examples," she began, "We hold regular monthly events where we feed homeless folks. We have a 'Day of Reason' on the 'Day of Prayer' at the capital to raise funds for organizations that help those who are precariously situated. Raising money for housing and such..."

"I didn't know your group was so community-focused. That's impressive."

"Well, we have to care for these people," she opined. "They are often told that *God* will take care of them, contingent of course," she added under her breath. "But that's not practical care. Oh, and we have a counter-protest on Easter at Planned Parenthood. But our most ambitious activism is currently working to change Minnesota laws so churches are not the only nonprofit that is able to conduct weddings."

I looked up from my notes. "That's a law?"

"Yes," she stated. "Currently, the only choices people have outside of religion are a judge or becoming clergy online and simply not reflecting religious beliefs in the ceremony."

"Are you married?" I interjected.

"Yes, I am."

"Is that what you did at your ceremony?"

Her voice went a bit hushed. "No. Unfortunately, my husband's father was dying from a brain tumor rapidly and we were married by his pastor." She looked down for a moment, causing her wavy hair to dangle.

"I'm sorry." There was a moment of silence. I picked up again, "What is your opinion on why there are so many strong believers in religion? Why do you think it's such a widely accepted concept?"

Stephanie didn't even pause before answering, "Sitting with the fact that there's a lot about the world that we don't know is uncomfortable," she answered. "But it's an important discomfort. It makes us think and question. Sexism, racism, how the world really works... if it were less uncomfortable, we wouldn't be here. But the discomfort pushes progress along."

"That's an interesting perspective."

"Also," Stephanie continued, "spiritual or metaphysical beliefs give answers. In my opinion, though, it's highly unlikely one of the competing 'answers' could be correct. I just think for many people, it's important that there *could* be an answer."

"That leads nicely to my next question. What would you say to someone who insists they've had a near-death experience and witnessed something supernatural?"

"Well, I have had some strange experiences in my life," she began with a slight shrug, "Like a Benadryl dream on the edge of sleep. Brains are capable of really amazing things. And when I wake up and try to explain what I experienced, it makes no sense at all. I expect that type of thing would also occur when a person is close to death. Strange things happen in the brain.

And if religion is a big part of your life's narrative, it might be the only way to make sense of it."

"So based on your opinion that it was all created within the brain, do you think it is still an important message for the person to process?" I asked.

"It can be important," she surmised. "I studied psychology and I do think, once interpreted, messages or dreams can give good info. But I don't think we should feel compelled to take messages from it. It may just be our brain lumping things together in a state of confusion, not anything larger."

"What do you think about the universe or fate or destiny or a collective conscious guiding us with signs or signals?"

"Guiding? No. I don't think there is any sort of active guiding process. There is a whole lot of world going on around us that we don't observe overtly. We could pick up information that we don't recognize and make a decision that plays out well. Or we can make our decision based on reason that doesn't end well. There is nothing trying to tell us which way is better—that's just ourselves... Existing is weird."

I smirked. "I agree. Well then, with no signs and no gods, what do you believe about a soul? Do you believe humans have a soul?"

"I don't," Stephanie answered. "I think that the feelings of soul and consciousness are emergent properties of our crazy brain. It's kind of wonderful we can feel all of this as a sack of fat-covered meat with electrical impulses!"

I laughed at the image. "I suppose it is. And what happens to us sacks when we die?"

"Bacteria has a heyday and then the bugs come in to clean up!" she replied. We both laughed again. "Entropy would be the term. Dust to dust..."

I looked up from my notes.

She added, "I know I just quoted the Bible, but that's the reality."

"With that being the reality that awaits you... are you afraid to die?"

Stephanie took in a large breath and held it a moment before answering. "I... don't know. As a person who has faced off with mental illness in the past, I know I do not want to die. There are things I want to do and accomplish and spend more time with. I'm afraid of not getting to do those things more than I'm afraid of ending."

"And what do you think about the belief in reincarnation? That you might be headed back down to do it all over again?"

"I think it was a completely rational belief when it came into being. I have had a few people remind me of other people. If I think about it, I don't feel like I will actually die... But to have existed as something else before I was born doesn't seem the case either. There are so many things about child development and personality changes that could challenge the belief as a whole. But I understand how some could hold a belief in reincarnation."

"Have you ever thought yourself to have lived before?" I asked.

Stephanie chuckled. "I may have had a casual recreational hypnosis experience," she said.

I laughed again. "Did you just say *casual recreational hypnosis*? I haven't heard that one before." Even as my laugh faded, I realized that was probably the exact term to define my experiences with past life regressions.

She went on. "Well, when I did, I came up with a personality, but there was nothing about it that I wouldn't have known already. And I write short fiction so..."

"That's just what my family said to me when I experienced

a past life personality," I agreed. "As writers, our imaginations are pretty active."

She agreed. "And sometimes it may not just be our imagination that creates these things."

"What do you mean? Have you had other supernatural experiences?"

"When I was two, I thought my grandparents' house was haunted."

"Oh," I replied, furiously writing. My brain was already wondering how a person who did not believe in souls could believe in ghosts. But my questions were quickly dispelled.

"I saw something. I'm sure I did," Stephanie explained. "It was like the motion of running across the doorway or tracking lights. And later, ghost hunting, I saw it again. In a life of insomnia, what I saw made an impression on me. It was sort of part of my story until I was a teenager. At that point, I realized how much work I was doing to imbue weird amorphous things with shape and meaning. I learned if I stopped doing that, I wouldn't interpret them as a ghost."

"Okay... so it wasn't a ghost?"

She shook her head. "In my thirties, I was diagnosed with a migraine syndrome that affects my side vision. I knew I had chronic migraines, but I didn't realize I was literally seeing things because of them. It could cause, among other things, seeing tracking lights. In the end, there was a perfectly logical explanation for a decade-long ghost story."

"Wow, it's refreshing to hear a rational explanation for one, honestly." I looked at my notes.

She nodded again.

"Well," I began, looking up at her looking at me through the screens. "I think that concludes my questions, unless there are any final thoughts you'd like to include?"

Stephanie thought a moment. "There are times I want this all to be true," she spoke with a more distant tone. "It's so important to people. And it's nice to think that this isn't it. I've just been thinking about naturalism versus supernaturalism since college, and unfortunately, I haven't found anything to make me believe atheism isn't true."

I paused, thinking it all over. "Thank you for your honesty. I think it's an opinion to contemplate. Yours was an interesting perspective to hear from."

She thanked me, I wished her luck on all of the upcoming activism and we ended the call that had been five months in the making.

After my interview with Stephanie, I stayed awake pondering *supernatural*. It was a word that defined much more than superheroes, aliens and ghosts. And being raised in a fairly intellectual, well-read family, it felt like something my siblings would tease me for "falling for."

It all reminded me of a comical, yet eye-opening experience my daughter had in kindergarten around Christmastime. A situation where, in our family at least, logic and reason had a mini battle with the supernatural... The Cookie Baby.

At age five, we seem to think children should believe in magic. "We" meaning the American cultural society. Believing in Santa Claus, flying reindeer, elf toymakers constructing a variety of toys that look an *awful lot* like the toys on the shelves in Target—we shovel it all into our children's maturing minds. And, hey, I am probably more guilty than most (my family literally calls me *Jingle Gina* that time of year), but I feel like there has to be a line drawn somewhere. My daughter wants to know how things work; she seems interested in mechanical and physical workings. I don't want to discourage that. So I'm quick to explain (okay, overexplain) how things work. This includes talking about what's real and what's not real.

With that backstory, it was a late December afternoon when I picked up my daughter from elementary school. As we were holding hands and walking back to my car a block away, parked in a snowbank, I noticed she had a funny look on her face. "How was school today?" I asked, looking down at her cherub cheeks peeking out from her fuzzy hat and scarf.

Her eyes got wide. "We read a book about a *gingerbread* man!"

"Okay..."

"And then he came alive and *jumped* out of the book!" she told me with animated hand gestures.

"Really?" I replied, unsure of how to respond.

We stopped to wait for the crossing guard. She squeezed my hand. "Mom, will characters in *my* books come alive and jump out of my books in my room while I'm sleeping?"

I laughed without meaning to. "No, honey."

"But that's just what happened at school! Mr. Johnson showed us Cookie Baby up on the wall by the ceiling! He got out while we were at music class."

I unlocked my car and tossed her backpack in the backseat between the two car seats. I hoisted my petite five-year-old over the snowbank and started buckling her while she continued her story. "Mr. Johnson said if we touch him, his magic will go away. He's bringing special gloves to school tomorrow so *he* can touch him..." she drifted off and stared at the sky. "He's really alive, Mom."

On our drive across town to pick up my son from

preschool, there was nonstop Cookie Baby talk; Cookie Baby being the name she had come up with for this character. I realized her teacher was attempting to do an "Elf on the Shelf" sort of scenario; a tradition our family had never participated in.

By the time the three-year-old was also in the car, the story had taken on a creepier vibe. "And then the Cookie Baby JUMPED out of the book while we were gone. He came alive! He did. And he's hanging up by the ceiling WATCHING us now."

"Honey," I chimed in over my shoulder, seeing my son hugging himself over the three-point harness. "Maybe it didn't really come alive. It's nothing to worry about. Maybe it was all just a story." At the time, I didn't know if I should just straight-out explain the "magic" or not. I opted not to. But that night while tucking her in, things got more intense.

I clicked off my daughter's light and sat on the edge of her bed to say goodnight. She was huddled in the covers, squeezing her beloved blankie, which she hadn't needed in months. "Are you okay, babe?" I asked her, brushing the hair from her forehead.

"Can you... can you take all those books out of here, please?" She pointed across the room.

"Oh, baby," I exhaled with a chuckle. I looked over at her packed-full bookshelf, then back to her. Her eyes were shimmering in the thin stream of light from the hallway. She was terrified.

I hugged her tight. "Listen, I'm thinking that Mr. Johnson was just telling a story. Characters can't come alive from a book or show. You know they are not real. They are stories made up from someone's imagination."

"Like unicorns?"

"Yes, just like unicorns. Not real."

She seemed to relax a bit and I said goodnight, shaking my head at Cookie Baby. But the next day, things were even more exaggerated.

"Cookie Baby IS real and he can use SCISSORS!" my daughter yelped the second I was in ear shot as I picked her up the next afternoon. She was petrified.

"What?"

"I told all the kids that Cookie Baby wasn't real and that Mr. Johnson was just making him up in his imagination so the kids tried to touch him. He was in a different place on the wall—he moved! When we went to art class, Mr. Johnson left his magic gloves on his desk so he could touch him when we got back, to show us he was really real. He locked the door with a key, mom!"

I was already making a face. This wasn't going well for us.

She continued. "When we came back from art, Mr. Johnson's magic gloves were chopped up! Cookie Baby *used scissors* to cut the fingers off the magic gloves! He did, Mom! He's alive! He must didn't want to be touched."

Shaking my head, I endured another ride home with *Cookie Baby: The Hell Rising* being told in the backseat to my son, who lapped up every word.

I talked with Craig about what to do. Was it okay to let her believe? Were we ruining things by explaining it? Was there such a thing as a healthy dose of magic?

In the end, I told her everything. Characters could not come alive, just like animals couldn't talk and dinosaurs weren't around anymore. She seemed to understand. But it took Christmas vacation to get the entire scenario out of our daily conversation.

Humans like stories. I understand that. And stories are best when shared. I was curious how my daughter would tell the tale next year. Would she include the part where she knew Mr. Johnson was the one moving the gingerbread baby or leave that out? Had I dampened her curiosity for the supernatural? And why did it seem that the most beloved and shared stories *were* about magic and unknown forces?

Maybe I should ask Cookie Baby.

While I was at my parents' house for Easter, I spent some time in my dad's home office with him. The owner of thousands of books and movies, his office is a chaotic room, with leaning shelves and stacks and piles. Eventually, he pulled out the entire series of *In Search Of*, a show I'd caught on The History Channel before. The series covered unexplainable, mysterious topics; made in the 1970s, hosted by a young Leonard Nimoy. I hadn't known the series I'd seen on TV was a reboot of an old show (which I usually pride myself on knowing).

"And the damn thing is," my father so eloquently stated, "They don't know anything now that they didn't know then! It's forty years later and we're still repeating the same things about the same mysteries. They just keep regurgitating the same points and counterpoints and no one's found the tiniest bit of new information on any of them."

I picked up the black-boxed set of DVDs. "One hundred forty-four episodes and they haven't moved forward on any of these topics? That seems hasty to claim."

He shook his head and left the room to refill his coffee cup. It was 10:00pm; my children were asleep, and we had a long day of coloring eggs and convincing my clever daughter that the Easter Bunny was real, just months after Cookie Baby.

My father came back into the living room with his steaming cup. "Well, pick one out then."

I smiled and sought one out that piqued my interest—scientists who believed they could photograph an aura. It reminded me of a thought I'd had in high school, which I'd written in bold, colorful lettering on my journal cover: *What if souls had a smell?* I had long been fascinated with the idea of being able to sense, smell or see something that "wasn't there."

We stayed up until almost 1:00am pondering the mysteries of the universe. I told myself it was for research.

Synchronicity & signs

BECAUSE OF ALL the examination I'd been doing about karma and laws of attraction and such, I found myself reading too much into things... at least, I think it was too much? One weekend in April, I attended a reunion party for a high school friend who was returning from a tour in Afghanistan. (Kinda put things into perspective.) The people attending were friends I hadn't seen in around a decade. Friends who had helped shape me. Friends I missed connecting with.

After a typical gathering, loud and fun with pizza and beer (which I did not partake in because of the new diet), the group pared down to a handful of us. We went back to a friend's parent's house—just like in high school days—and the conversation went deeper.

Normally, I don't talk about the book I'm working on while in the process. I try to only jump into it if someone presses. I'm sure it's no surprise that the topic of souls and reincarnation and a spirit world is enough to make some people's eyes glaze over (which literally happened to my sister at this party when I was asked to explain the project). But after giving the elevator pitch about my project, my friends wanted to know more. More about my past life stories, more about the upcoming interviews, more about the percentages of people out there with like ideas and beliefs. I hadn't thought about putting together percentages of beliefs, but agreed to do so. They also inspired me to put my full past life write-ups at the end of the book for those interested in the fine details of what I experienced.

One friend, Adam, mentioned that a classmate of his was now a neuropsychologist. Since Adam was a sophomore when I was a senior, I always saw his class as much younger. I was surprised to hear about his friend-turned-neuropsychologist. And I wondered if it was the woo-woo telling me to reach out. Because, while I had little issue with cold-emailing a stranger living in a different country, messaging someone I went to high school with but never spoke to seemed more anxiety-inducing.

Additionally, back in the late 1990s, Adam introduced me to an album that resonated with me from moment one. Just before I was invited to attend the reunion party, I had found the CD from Adam stuck inside an old, sun-melted CD case in the bottom of a box, after our basement flooded thanks to the immense spring thaw. I hadn't seen the CD in just about as long as I hadn't seen Adam, but I'd been listening to it on repeat and relearning my love of the music.

One of the songs—I always assumed was about love—chanted the words, "there'll be no end" and "we'll never say goodbye." It was stuck in my head. And the words held a new double meaning to me. I listened to it every time I got in the car. It gave me visible goosebumps when I sang along. I decided to try it out on my son. I had the volume high and was singing my heart out. Halfway through the song, I looked in the rearview mirror to see him with his pouty lip out. "What's wrong?" I asked him over my shoulder. "This is too sad. I don't want this song," was his reply.

So it wasn't just me. It was a damn moving song.

Was it a coincidence that I found the CD from Adam right before I saw him for the first time in seven years? Or a sign?

Next, our household endured a string of events that people seemed to conclude was "bad luck." Never a true subscriber of the concept of luck, I admit I see how thin a line exists between luck, karma and woo-woo. An example? Craig ran to the store at 9:00pm to get medicine for the three-year-old, only to have the gas tank fall off of his vehicle. Yes, right off the undercarriage. He coasted into a parking spot, sparks flying, only to have several emergency vehicles hose down the Target parking lot like a hazard scene. This was after new tires, new brakes and a new muffler on the vehicle just months prior. Needless to say, he returned without the medicine and needed my car the next day, but I was home with a sick preschooler anyway, so I guess that portion worked out.

I was feeling burned out and exasperated at how many things had gone wrong when a friend tried to cheer me up by reminding me to "enjoy the sunshine." The weather had gone from a freak April snow day to dreary rain to mildly sunny. Thanks to a sleepover in my home office with the kids, a fleece Batman blanket was covering the window, plus the curtains, plus the blinds. I unclipped the clothespins (it was a serious tent-making sleepover), took down the heavy blanket, opened the curtains and pulled the blinds. And there, chirping noisily, was a beautiful red cardinal.

He was on a branch at eye level with me, being in the second story window. He looked right at me and stayed long enough for me to snag a photo. He sang for a little while before taking flight. I had heard cardinals were a sign, but didn't know what kind. I looked it up and found a couple options, one being a sign of reassurance. And frankly, after our myriad of bad things, that was nice.

Ten hours later, I arrived home, exhausted with a trunk full of groceries. I pulled into the driveway and there he was again, but in a different tree, chirping away and looking right at me again. It was a strange feeling to be noticed by a bird. But sometimes the smallest things are the greatest things. It was just the boost I needed.

I checked my email to see a positive reply from the psychic medium that Aileen had connected me with. I was excited and nervous. I had never spoken to a person with purported psychic abilities. The idea made me a little uneasy.

With a win under my belt, I looked up the high school classmate-turned-neuropsychologist. He looked the same. I found his contact information, but never composed the message to him. I hoped that I wasn't asking, receiving and then disregarding. There was probably a soul penalty for that. Would it mess up my track record? Would it throw off my whole project to skip an interview I was led to?

I didn't know. But sometimes high school awkwardness ruled all.

In the fourth week of my nutrition program, I attempted my first-ever three-day fast. Fasting was something that seemed synonymous with balance and spiritual health. Ghandi came to mind. Or Buddha meditating under a tree. But I'll admit, this was not what mine looked like. Mine was less about balance and more about stubborn will. In sum, Craig said I was in the kitchen more during that month than he had ever seen in all our years combined. At my core, change was occurring. And while I had more energy and more weight loss, I wanted more.

A fast suggested that was possible. But even with my fast being less than spiritual, I hoped I would have some sort of enriching experience.

And then I did, but it wasn't related to the mind/body balance. It was related to a rekindled connection.

Back in college, I worked at a big box store to pay the bills. We all wore nametags with first names spelled out in sticker letters. One day, a manager came up and asked me how Michelle and I were related. "Michelle who?" I'd asked, not even knowing which employee he meant. He made a funny face and replied, "But you both have the same crazy last name..."

After rushing home to my father the genealogist, he was disheartened to learn I didn't have a clue who she was. She was my second cousin. We were the same age. Grew up mere miles apart. Had met as kids.

For a while after that, Michelle and I hung out—went to the lake together, to parties with our coworkers—but I didn't last long at the store. This being the days before one tap of a touchscreen could link you eternally through the internet, (I'm not even sure we had cell phones yet. Oh, the horrors.) leaving the store meant losing touch with Michelle. But everything about working at the giant retailer went against my beliefs. In fact, after filling timecards with days of watching training videos on the perils of unions, I started asking around about why we didn't have one, and what would happen if we tried to start one. Needless to say, management didn't like that. I was asked to write an essay making a case to keep my job (yes, seriously). Instead, I eloquently stated why I could no longer work there.

After just five months, I quit, leaving behind a note stuck to the underside of the front desk that merely stated, "Ours is not to question why. Ours is but to do or die." A play on the words of Alfred, Lord Tennyson. As I was nineteen, it felt poignant.

In the present day, I was in the weight loss nutrition program with a handful of other people from Minnesota. We were all connected on social media. And, after fourteen years, there was Michelle in the list of women participating in the program. In fact, she had started it the very same day as I had. We were the newcomers to the group.

We started texting, reconnecting and checking in on each other throughout the program.

We began our fast at 5:30pm on a Monday, not planning to have food again until 5:30pm on Thursday—the longest by far I'd ever gone without eating. It started out fine. A little hunger, but nothing terrible. But then I started making rookie mistakes. I "supported" my fast with lemon ginger water, tea and bone broth. I have family and friends who fast and they were quick to tell me that any flavor in the mouth caused the digestive system to get excited, which translated into more growling and more hunger pains. Day one was not easy for me.

Day two of the fast was my daughter's sixth birthday. If I had planned it, that wouldn't have been my choice. But it just happened that it landed in week four of my program. Michelle also had a child's birthday to survive without a morsel, but she wisely started her fast after the birthday treats.

My plan was to get plenty of sleep and sleep through the hunger. But at 4:00am, my son came in crying that his ear hurt too badly to sleep. He'd had a cold for more than a week, so it was no surprise, but unfortunate timing to be awake those extra hours with him. We all spent the morning of our daughter's birthday in Urgent Care for his ear infection. I was a zombie.

Though our nutrition group promised mental clarity and

less hunger, forty-eight hours in, I was nervous about my upcoming interview (and all of the stupid mistakes I'd been making all day).

Trust yourself.
Trust your ability.

The Psychic Medium

I MET MELISSA Divine on a nondescript street in a nondescript house in town. Though she wasn't from the same town, she traveled in to give readings.

Melissa agreed to meet me at a Float and Healing Center. After reading up on the meeting location, I realized it was literally a place to go and float in a tank. A list of health benefits were among the reasons individuals floated, but another reason, per the center's website, was to "reach the elusive theta brainwave state (similar to long-term meditators) by remaining in a sensory-deprived setting for around an hour or more."

Captivating—both because it was somewhat pertinent to my journey, but also because the reason Melissa was meeting me at the float center was that it was owned by her partner. (Can you imagine that Meet Cute?) But the thought of being trapped in a tank of darkness, all alone with my thoughts, unable to do anything... not for me. In fact, it made me think of the horrible medical test Cecilia had been forced to attempt. (HOOYAH.)

So my growling stomach and I met Melissa at our predetermined time. It had been particularly frenzied getting to the interview at 5:00pm, but I ended up being a few minutes early. When I arrived at the yellow door, I was greeted by Melissa.

Her golden blonde hair curled near her ears and her blue eyes sparkled as she invited me in.

"This is Jon Maki, the owner of the Float and Healing Center," she introduced once we were inside. Jon was tall with blonde hair and was wearing a branded Float T-shirt. I wondered if he was technically on the clock. They invited me to sit in the main lounge of the healing center, which was filled with peaceful greens and palm-fronded plants. Calming music played from somewhere overhead. I sat in an arm chair near the window.

After I'd thanked them for meeting with me and filled them in on the interview plan, I was excited to begin the interview (and stop thinking about how good pizza would taste... not very Zen of me).

The windows were all open, letting in a fresh April breeze. It was finally spring in Minnesota. It was an ideal setting for a deep soul conversation. Melissa sat on the edge of the long sectional sofa's chaise facing me.

"The best place to start," I said with a smile, "is the beginning. What is your spiritual background that led you to today?"

Melissa smiled back. "That's a complicated story," she began. "But I suppose it is for everyone?"

I nodded. "Most people begin with how they were raised. Did you attend church?" I offered.

"Yes, I grew up in a small Midwestern town; raised Lutheran. But I clearly remember sitting in church—somewhere around the age of three to six—and listening to the service thinking, 'These people don't get it.' I began poking holes at a young age."

Her comment made me think of my own children, aged

three and six, and wonder if they had already had thoughts on such grand topics.

"That said," she continued, "I wasn't consciously aware of my abilities until my thirties."

I made a face. I didn't mean to, but I was astonished. I had always assumed someone identifying as a psychic medium would have just always known about their abilities. "Wow..." I muttered, looking up from my yellow notepad.

"To clarify," she continued, "I think I just called them different things." She lifted her hands in preparation for making air quotes. "I *had good gut instincts* and was *good at reading body language*, that sort of thing. My abilities were there, but I just called them more socially acceptable names." Melissa's eyes took on a different look. "My father passed away... suddenly and tragically."

"I'm sorry," I blurted as if by instinct.

She nodded in acceptance and continued, "At that point, I went to see a medium as a client. I had an intense curiosity once I lost someone to figure out if it was all real—the crossing over. I went in with my mother and sister. I think we went in with a healthy skepticism, looking for the proverbial signs, but I was intoxicatedly enthralled." She paused and crossed her arms in her lap. No longer looking at me, but looking to the side, she continued, "That first reading blew me away," she said. "There was evidence that proved to me beyond a doubt that we were communicating with my father."

I looked up again. Melissa looked a little sad. Jon was in the other room, but came in to sit on the couch with Melissa. I felt a strong sense of compassion in the room.

Melissa took a breath and crossed her legs, passing a small smile to Jon. She elaborated, "Serendipity brought me to mediumship."

"I love that word," I told her. "I wanted to ask you about signs in the universe."

"I have plenty of stories about them!" she answered. "At the end of my undergrad degree, I was doing a research paper. An internet search brought up an ad for a mediumship website that was very compelling. Through a series of events, it all led me to England at an intensive course to hone in on psychic skills. I felt so drawn and called, but I was afraid people would laugh at me. *'Poor American, she thinks she can give a reading'* type of thing. On day one, we walked in and were seated opposite a stranger and told, 'Okay, give them a reading.'"

"And did you?" I jumped in, eager to know if that's when she discovered her ability.

She smiled. "I did. I knew specifics—the type of boat his father had, his love of poetry..."

I was nodding along. I glanced over to see Jon also enthralled. I wondered if she had told him this story before. "So is that when you became a psychic medium?" I asked.

"Well, it required a lot more synchronicities before I believed I could do it."

"Such as?"

She chuckled. "Such as passing a literal billboard that said, *'Psychics Needed. You know where to apply.'* while considering going to school in England. Hence the *you know where to apply* part. The very next road sign contained the name of my school in England; it just so happened to be the name of the town coming up. A third sign for a "crossover ahead" reminded me of a show I loved so I knew with all these very clear road signs in quick succession that Spirit wanted me to go to England."

My smile was incredulous. I wanted to know where that billboard was.

She continued with a renewed excitement in her story,

"Developing psychics have the connection, but don't have the trust," she stated in a teacherly tone. "I had to do a lot of research—really buckle down and teach myself psychic development through backs of bookstores and attending workshops."

"Can you explain more what you mean by *psychic*?"

Her blue eyes looked into mine. "Generically speaking, intuition is gut instinct; that feeling that something is really good or completely uncomfortable. It's not predicting that in six years you will get a great job. It's your spirit communicating with souls who have crossed over. Angels and spirit guides. Mediumship is communication with loved ones who've passed over. It's..." She brought her hands up and started mimicking tossing items out into the air in front of her. "It's telepathy and signs and signals and colors and needs," she listed, gesturing with each. "And sometimes I see them. A soul can choose how it will appear to a medium. But I don't always see them."

"When you're receiving the messages from them you actually see the deceased person?" I asked the amazing woman sitting across from me.

"An example," she began, "A soul appears to me as a seven-year-old girl. The soul is depicting how she wishes me to see her. Each psychic has different senses, like sight or touch, that they communicate best with. Some are strong at hearing. My strongest sense is *feeling*," she emphasized. "Feeling and emotions are my forte. I sense when they are coming close to me... I can sense personality. For instance, a young man around twenty years old came to me. His personality came through while I was doing a reading for his parents, who were in their fifties. He was touching my shoulder and leaning over me real close." She touched her own shoulder, then smiled. "I said to his parents, 'you have a real charmer here,' which they instantly related to. That was his flirty personality. Another example," Melissa continued, enjoying the opportunity to share her experiences, "was a reading I gave regarding someone's grandmother. It was as if she was giving me a tour of her home! I sensed standing in shag carpet in sandals. I could *feel* the shag carpet soft on my feet."

"Amazing..." I stammered, shaking my head a bit. It was a lot to take in. The woman sitting across from me was alleging that she could communicate with the spirit world. Meaning, in her opinion, there was no question that humans had souls and those souls could communicate with us.

As if she could sense a touch of skepticism creeping into my thoughts, she leaned in to give another story.

"One of my favorite stories of a skeptic-turned-believer is of a man over the phone. His wife booked a reading for him because she wanted—well I won't go into details, but she wanted a psychic to side with her!" She chuckled. "Over the phone, he started our conversation by saying, 'I hope you know I am a total skeptic.' To which I replied, 'Let's just see what happens.' Five or ten minutes in, I was describing the home his parents lived in. I knew more than things a person could google. I could explain his parents—who they were and how they lived their lives; repeating a few of his deceased father's bad jokes. 'Oh my God, this is real,' he said to me. Not long after, he ended up booking two more readings. I think he became consciously ready."

"Ready for receiving the message you mean?"

She elaborated. "Well, I believe a person needs to be ready and open to receiving the message, but also ready for the content *of* the message. I'm sure you've had moments in your life where you've received advice or wisdom, but it wasn't until much later that you thought back and *realized* the weight of it. We must be ready."

"So is the main reason people come to you to ask about a loved one who has passed away? They are seeking the messages?"

She nodded. "Learning how to heal and move past circumstances is vital. I know that firsthand. My father's death was horrific for me... violent for him. But I was able to heal. Mainly, knowing that his soul goes on and that he didn't suffer. I think we need to know that so we don't move forward with dread and fear for our own time. Seeking out my father and communicating with him did two important things for me," she detailed, learning toward me. "One, it took away the pain and hurt of his passing. And two, it completely altered my perspective of death." She let out an easy laugh and sent a look toward Jon. "Though if you sit next to me on an airplane, I'll still be terrified. A phobia is a phobia. But death is so different to me now."

I chimed in, "I honestly have felt the same. Almost immediately after my first past life regression, I realized I feared death far less."

She nodded, but expanded, "Yes, but mine goes even farther than that!" She nearly smirked at herself. "My mom called me two days ago to tell me a great uncle had passed on. I knew she wanted and expected me to be sad. But in my mind, I was nearly cheering! Congrats, Uncle, you completed your journey and you're off to the spirit world to see how you did. I know that may not sound like a common reaction, but I often feel like I should congratulate people for completing their mission."

I was smiling when I asked, "What did you mean that they are off to see how they did? Is it like the movie, *Defending*

Your Life, where they have to watch a replay of their earthly actions?"

"I don't know that one," Melissa replied. "But, from what I've gathered from the spirits, there is a life review after we die. But it's not reliving our life through our own eyes. It's from the perspective of *others*. How we affected others. We can *feel* what our words and actions felt like to them," she emphasized.

My eyes widened. True or not, that was a code to live by. Treat others like you will have to feel how you made them feel someday.

Heavy.

I looked at my notes and continued. "So, does that mean you believe in reincarnation?"

"Yes, I think of reincarnation as a traditional education. We take tests, learn lessons, become more intelligent... and then it's summer vacation. So, we come back the next time to learn more lessons, take more tests, advance to the next grade. It's never the same lessons. And," she added quickly, "it seems like most people come to want to learn more about this topic at right around the same age—like thirty-four, thirty-five, thirty-six," she said.

I found it amusing that I was both in that age bracket when I began this book, and had come to the same conclusion thanks to the general audience of those weird and wise Facebook groups. Also, her description echoed that of Aileen's: lessons and soul goals. "Do you know any of your past lives?"

Melissa tucked her legs up under her to sit cross legged. "Yes, and it was a lesson to be learned. I saw myself as some sort of a guard in a prison a long time ago. Most of the prisoners were being sold into slavery. I knew I tortured them for entertainment; had no cares about how I treated them." She paused. "But I know I chose that life. I chose that hard lesson to learn.

I credit this for giving me a heightened sense of compassion in this lifetime. I came out of it being a soul who is greatly in tune with how my actions affect others; highly intuitive about how others feel."

My mind was connecting dots between Pooja's Hindu-inspired statement about how "we have all been murderers," and Aileen's comment about Jeffrey Dahmer. They seemed to be etching out the same picture.

Already having mentioned my chat with Aileen, I said, "Aileen heard a theory that once a person or soul is deemed evil—her example was Jeffrey Dahmer—it is shattered into pieces that are then absorbed into everyone else, making it impossible for that bad spirit to exist again."

Melissa flung her hands out in front of her, "Eww, I don't want to think there's a piece of Jeffrey Dahmer in me!" She laughed and then resituated herself.

I shrugged.

"But that's an interesting theory. I haven't heard that one."

"Do you believe in karma?" I asked, building on the topic of good versus evil.

"In a way. I do believe that we are all connected and affecting one another." She linked her fingers together in front of her. "Like cogs in a clock, everything must be perfectly lined up and timed before it will work. My part affects your part." She pointed to me. "And if he does something different, it throws us all off." She looked to Jon. "Like maybe Jon and I would have found each other sooner if he had moved on from his divorce faster." She looked back to me. "Maybe we held up this very book by delaying the whole timeline."

"That's a lot of pressure," I inserted. "That's a lot of responsibility, being the reason other people aren't able to complete their soul mission."

"Well, our spirit guides are able to assist on some level," Melissa reassured.

"How so?"

"Well, we group ourselves with souls based on our intended lessons. Our teammates—the other souls in our soul group, soul family, or team—help us accomplish our goals. Like a coach on the sidelines, sometimes they regroup and offer signs and advice to the players. They are sometimes able to stop us from doing the wrong thing. Like they make things so uncomfortable it shakes us to our core. There are times in our lives when we need them strongly. Just like the members of a team, they are all different. And if some are tired, they sit on the sidelines and others jump in. They might be a mailman or a teacher we once had. They're making plays and getting exhausted. They have unique traits and skills. In my group, one is like, 'hello, you're psychic!' in a tough love manner. Some are pushy and don't take no for an answer. Some are loving, like my father."

I didn't hide my shock. "Your father's in your soul group? You communicate with him regularly?" I asked.

She smiled. "He's sort of like my coworker."

I was shaking my head again. An astounding thing to imagine; communicating on a daily basis with a loved one who had passed.

She continued, "I'd say I'm closer to him now than I was when he was physical... but... gosh, it would be so nice to just touch my dad's hand again."

I felt my brow furrow in sadness. There was a strange tragic quality to a relationship such as that. "I haven't lost anyone close to me, thankfully. I'm not sure I would have that kind of person in my soul group."

Melissa let out a small laugh and was shaking her head, "They know *you*. All of them know you and are cheering for you! Even if you've never met, they are interested in your life. They knew you as a soul and are interested and even invested in your life plans. What benefits you, benefits them. They show up for you."

"What a thought..."

The red flowers on Melissa's shirt flowed in a breeze from the open window. "What comes across in the messages I've received is that there is a throng of spiritual people to meet you once you are taken out of your physical body. Spirit often depicts it for me as souls in a circle around you, with one soul as the lead; the first person to see you when you pass. The circle huddles with the person every step of the transition. Not once have I heard words like scary or lonely or dark. All indications make it seem like there is a great deal of effort and care to prepare for the person's arrival. It is exactly like the soul wants it. The group took great care to prepare the space. Think of it like a baby shower," she offered. "Preparing for a new life to come to Earth, except the spirits do that for us before we go there."

"Wow..." I muttered once again.

Melissa smiled and wagged a finger at me. "Yeah, so think about what you want to see when you arrive. Because they will have it all ready for you!"

"That sounds similar to what I read in *90 Minutes in Heaven*," I began, setting aside my yellow notepad for a moment. "He arrives and sees the gates of Christian Heaven, is surrounded by loving spirits and hears and sees angels. But he was a minister leaving a Baptist convention when he nearly died."

"To me, that simply means that's what he wanted it to be. That's what would make the most sense to him; ease him through the transition."

"Uh-huh," I said, tapping my pen on my lips. "I read that

book right after researching Buddhism, which is 'less is more' in most of their approaches. I got stuck on the fact that in *90 Minutes in Heaven*, Piper hears a constant, almost deafening sound of angels singing God's praise. Which, if I understand correctly, is almost opposite of what a Buddhist would say our creator would need or want."

"Souls have the ability to alter the experience," Melissa offered.

I nodded. "So going back to my original list of questions, how does this translate into your personal beliefs? Are you afraid of death?" I literally started writing the word *no*, assuming I already knew the answer. But you know what they say about assuming.

"Yes... and no," Melissa replied. "Am I afraid of my own death? No. Am I afraid of suffering? Yes. Am I afraid of losing someone else close to me? Yes. Sure, I have home videos of my dad, and I'm able to communicate with him. But to see and hear him is something very different. The human experience of my dad is so different than the spiritual, even though I communicate with him nearly every day."

"I just have to ask," I began, now leaning in toward her.

Melissa cut me off with a lifted palm, "Let me guess, do spirits bombard me until I walk up to strangers and give them messages like the Long Island Medium?"

I laughed. "Not what I was going to ask, but now that you brought it up—how does that work?"

"I have been very up front about my abilities with Spirit—Spirit being the proper noun for the collective of all souls in the spirit world," she added. "I've informed them that I will not be *open* all of the time. I have boundaries. Does that stop all of the messages? No. But it curbs them."

"So there *are* times you walk up to strangers and give them messages from deceased loved ones?"

"I try not to," she said with a small head shake. "For example, one day I was shopping at a grocery store. I was going up an aisle and an older lady was going down the aisle. As our carts passed, I heard her husband whisper that I should tell her that he thought she looked pretty in her pink sweater. I did not. But in the next aisle, we crossed paths again. Again, he insisted that I pay her a compliment because she was lonely. I didn't. But the third time I walked past her, he told me she lived alone and was missing the sense of touch. Missing him. So as I passed her, I told her how pretty she looked in her pink sweater. She smiled a grateful smile."

"So you did it, but on your own terms," I concluded.

"Right."

"That brings up the questions I was going to ask. I was wondering if it's terribly exhausting having this much communication on a daily basis—the spirits, the messages, the mediumship..."

"It can be a lot," she agreed. "While I'm working as a healer or psychic, I'm also working on myself. It is exhausting, but so rewarding. Many times, people come to me after a trauma. But the overarching theme I communicate to them is beautiful. They come needing compassion and understanding and healing. And they receive it. But the healers need that as well. It's..." she trailed off, searching for the right words. "Beautiful and frustrating. I can't sweep my own stuff under the rug. And I'm more sensitive. I can't get away with not dealing with my own issues... I'm a completely different person because of it."

"So having direct access like you do, does that mean you are consciously aware of your soul mission?"

"We all have lessons and progress to make," she replied.

"Why accomplish everything right away? I think a big portion of what the soul needs to accomplish can be found on a not-to-do-list."

I smiled, liking the term.

"It's so much more about connections with other souls, not money spent on our kids or material items we're chasing. Things at a big, universal level. But why complete the mission and leave all of these experiences?"

Again, I loved the accidental flow of the interviews. From Pooja's Hindu explanation of the experiences we were here for, to Kitty and her passion for music and human experiences, to Audrey who celebrated all that was human. To have met so many people who recognized the importance of experiencing... After a pause, I looked back to my next question for Melissa. "So once the person dies and the soul leaves the body—and we will hope they completed their soul mission—is that when you can reach them and communicate with them?"

"Well, before I get to that, I want to challenge your assumption that the soul doesn't leave the body until death."

I arched an eyebrow.

She continued. "I have been informed by spirits that it's possible for the soul to leave a body *before* death; clinically before a body is pronounced dead."

"Okaaay..." I uttered, prompting her to elaborate.

"If you've ever spoken to someone with Alzheimer's or dementia, you know they have good days and bad days; days they are 'here' and days they are 'there.' When they are 'there,' they are learning the ropes and getting acquainted. And I don't think of 'there' as another place, but rather another dimension. The spirits I communicate with have made it seem like time is not linear and 'there' actually is 'here,' meaning, there are other dimensions of us living at the same time. Like I could be living in Egypt in the past at the same moment I am in my living room speaking to you."

A heavy concept. I made a note to tell Pooja. It was another way of explaining simultaneous lives.

"I remember one specific, graphic example of a mother coming to me after her daughter had been murdered," Melissa continued. "The mother was tortured by the idea that her daughter had been tortured. The daughter's spirit told me that she had been taken out of the physical body before the time of death, much to the relief of her mother... and all of us."

The sound of sputtering water within the small fountain on a shelf beside me suddenly took over the space. After a moment, the next song in the overhead music came on, a chanting, chiming tune.

"But to answer your question," Melissa said, "there is no need to wait until a certain time. I don't think there are any limits on spirit communication... except our own fears and limiting beliefs."

We were well over an hour into our interview. We continued talking about soul groups, the spirit world and twin flames—which she believed she and Jon were. She mentioned a scientific experiment where people in different countries were asked to complete the same puzzle. Once several had been completed, the new groups became faster at completing the puzzle—making a case for some sort of universal knowledge or consciousness that allowed for knowledge of the puzzle they shouldn't have had. Jon came in from the other room to join us. "Are there any final points you'd like to add from your point of view?" I asked, after nearly another hour of chatting about various topics.

"Actually, yes," Melissa stated. "I want to emphasize that

everybody can do this. Everyone can communicate with the spiritual world in some regard. It's a component of the soul to be able to connect to a divine consciousness—or however you'd like to verbalize it. We are all born with what I call *soul equipment*. Just like a musical talent, some are born with a stronger natural talent, some are able to learn at a fast pace, some are born with birth defects that make it impossible to really play, but it's always there. We sense this. But we don't trust it. It's only an ability if we don't explain it away. Anyone and everyone can have a moment of connection with someone who has passed. In fact, they do! They have a moment where a sight or sound or occurrence makes then wonder if it's a message from their loved one. My advice is to pause and feel... because it *is*. Trust that it is."

Since he was in the room with us, I turned to Jon. "Do your views align with hers on this topic?"

"For the most part," Jon said. "I got into floating for somewhat similar reasons," he motioned toward the back of the healing center where the float tanks were housed. "When I first tried it, I was bogged down with 3D issues."

I knew by 3D he was referring to states of consciousness. I'd learned that 3D was the physical and somewhat selfish point of view, as opposed to 4D, when you felt connected to a whole, or even 5D, when you ascended life's daily grit and existed in a pure state.

Jon continued, "When I was floating in the tank, I felt such a strong sense of 'Why are you living like this?' After that, I wanted to do it again so bad that I tried filling an outdoor hot tub with Epsom salt to float under the night sky. But it just wasn't the same. I started this Float and Healing Center because I feel like floating forces you to face your higher self.

It's a tool for heightening intuition and correcting one's self. We need to heal. And the tank meets a person where they are."

"Wow… have you tried it?" I asked Melissa.

"I have."

"And how often do you float?" I asked, turning back to Jon.

"A couple times a week. I go in seeking answers and usually find that out-of-the-blue solutions come into my head while I'm in there."

"How did you ever come across the idea of floating for healing?" I asked.

Jon chuckled. "As a kid, I watched the movie *Altered States*. It made an impact. I was curious about it and sensory-deprived states and consciousness. But I grew up in Hawaii and I was just sort of led to it." He stood up. "Do you want a quick tour?"

"Sure!" I said, standing for the first time in hours that had slipped by like minutes.

Jon led us to a back room. He opened the door and I couldn't believe the sight. Hung on the wall was the same expansive canvas print of a rope bridge in the jungle that hung in my bedroom at home. The canvas was more than five feet across and took up most of a wall.

"I have the same print hanging at home!" I practically yelped.

Jon and Melissa smiled and exchanged a look. I looked over to the enormous white tank in front of me. "So you climb into that?"

Jon smiled again. He was easy to talk to and had a very calming presence. "It's filled with Epsom salt and magnesium, very healing. When you're in there, it's completely dark with the door closed. It's your choice if you'd like to have music on during, but I generally turn it back on near the end to help people come out of the meditative state slowly."

I was nodding. The tank in front of me took up most of the room. I looked back to Jon. "And you fit in there?"

He chuckled. "Yes, all six-foot-five of me. It's large enough that I can sit up in there." He opened the white metal door. "There's a light in there too to use until you're situated." He shut the door and faced me. "I think you should do it!"

I felt my face flush and backed away toward the doorway where Melissa was standing. "No, no, I don't think so, thank you."

We all walked back to the main room to say our goodbyes. I felt compelled to give a reason. "I'm not claustrophobic, but the idea of doing nothing, alone in there for an hour, in silence... worst nightmare." I laughed at myself. Melissa gave me a look I interpreted as "we should unpack that," but she didn't say anything.

"Melissa had to do it with the door open the first time because she doesn't like confined spaces."

She nodded. Instead of gesturing toward the door, she sat again on the couch. I accepted the invitation to linger and let my inner AskHole thrive. She spoke a bit about it being good to be the different one in life. I mentioned in a joking tone about my Rh negative blood type, referring to the possibility I was probably part alien and thus knew all about being different. Instead of laughing at my sarcasm or asking what I meant, Jon's eyebrow hiked up to his hairline in intrigue and Melissa just nodded. It was the type of moment when Shaggy would proclaim to his sleuthing pup sidekick, "Zoinks, Scoobs!"

I opted to change the subject.

"You know," I started, on a more instigative topic, "I asked one of my previous interviewees if they thought there was a point where religion became harmful. The person said yes. I thought they were going to suggest history's religious crusades and executions or something along those lines, but instead, the interviewee replied, 'It crosses the line when it's someone claiming to be a psychic and taking peoples' hard-earned money.' How would you reply to something like that?"

Melissa didn't seem offended in the least. "My personal response would be that I believe in letting people have their own belief system. They are learning lessons and giving hope and being a part of a community. They will have a greater understanding of how the soul goes on when they're ready. Atheists and Catholics and everyone all cohabitating. Putting out positive loving energy."

"That sounds like my idea of Heaven," I mumbled. "But speaking of Catholics and this utopian afterworld... what's your take—or the spirits' opinion—on suicide?"

Once I'd asked the words, I wondered if I should have. But Melissa took on the question with confidence. "I actually have first-hand experience with that topic," she began. "After my divorce, my first husband chose to take his own life."

Sheepishness took over. I slumped in my seat a little, too awkward to grab my notepad again, but terribly curious about the answer.

She continued, "Humans have free will. And our spirit guides cannot prevent bad things from happening. They can make things uncomfortable and hope that will push us in a different direction, but they cannot prevent. But more than that, I believe suicide is a great spiritual and physical sacrifice. Think about all of the lives the action touches—the family, friends, community, church. A suicide could just be a component of a soul's lesson. Perhaps one that the person even selected with the aid of their wise soul group." She tuned back into me, shaking off the drifted off look that had come over her. "But if you're asking if they are there in the spirit world—yes, they are. We all are. Everyone is."

After my interview with Melissa and Jon, I hatched a plan to experience both a psychic medium reading and a float. Knowing my cousin Becky had always been interested in the idea of communication with spirits, I asked her if she would sign up for a reading with Melissa that I could attend and include in the book. She agreed without reservation. And as for the float tank, I knew just the person to ask.

On one of the last days of April, I woke up at 4:09am. I know it was exactly that time because the Beach Boys started playing in my mind. Though normally vigilant about getting a healthy number of hours of sleep each night (which experts agree is in the range of seven to nine hours per night for the average adult), I had stayed up until midnight researching. After a long time mentally hosting a high school-style debate about the pros and cons of getting out of bed, I gave up and went into my office to write. It was dark outside, but the birds were already singing. The weekend's freak snow showers had melted away again and spring was all around. In the darkness out the window, I could see the new buds on the tree silhouetted by the orangish streetlamp outside.

My first task was to email Pooja in India to tell her about the theories I had collected for her—Aileen's mention of higher souls being able to split, and Melissa's talk about being in different dimensions at the same time.

As it was afternoon in India, I received her reply right away:

"Wow, Gina! This is so interesting. I can totally relate to the theory of time not being linear, brings lot of conviction to how I feel about time and dimensions. I can't explain how these two theories have brought clarity to my "what was that" experiences. I have heard this term "twin flames," but am now going to read more on this. If there can be twin, then there may be multiple flames too. If there are multiple flames, then it's equivalent to the second theory of living in different dimensions at the same time. Wow! You've made it very simple to understand by connecting links. Thanks for finding time to write to me. I am feeling fountain of energy now!"

It was not even 5:00am, yet I felt the fountain, too. One of the effects of losing eleven pounds in a month was apparently not being able to sleep. At least, I thought that was the reason. Though it could have just been pure excitement. Because, really, I was excited! My journey had been nothing like I imagined at the beginning. In fact, nearly my entire outline was obsolete. But it was more beautiful. More messy and organic and enlightening. It grew into a collection of remarkable humans capable of astonishing things. And though I agreed with every person along the way who told me it was ambitious and a large idea to tackle, I was so grateful I did it anyway.

I was excited because so many opportunities fell into place. It felt like I stepped up to a door and it opened by itself. Suddenly, I saw the end of the book. And it was a grand finale! Many had asked how I would know when I was done. How many interviews I would conduct? How many months I would study? I didn't know the answer until that morning.

At the end of the week, I would be in Memphis. Beyond my

excitement for a vacation with the love of my life and the new culture and music—I was so curious to see how Memphis *felt*.

After my first past life vision of Jean in Canada, I spent weeks trying to zero in on the mountainous area where he spent his happy life. I thought about planning a trip to Quebec, as his message was my first. But Memphis just came to me. It was given to me like a gift. Craig certainly wasn't thinking about Sweet Bea, my past life vision from the 1960s, when he hunted down tickets to the music festival. And now I would have a location to search in mere days.

Also, I was excited that Melissa Divine agreed to allow me to sit in on a psychic reading with my cousin. I was excited to hear it, watch it, feel it. I was excited Becky might have the chance to connect with the spirit of her father—my uncle—who had impacted our lives tremendously with his big heart and big humor. I was so grateful that both Melissa and Becky were accepting of me lurking on the sidelines, taking notes, hiding behind my garish yellow paper and chicken scratch writing.

And I could not stop wondering how Craig would fare in the float tank. As someone who has not spent a lot of time pondering spiritual questions, I was curious what his experience would be like. Would he be moved? Would he find answers? Would he receive? Or would he just lie there, floating in the darkness, relieved by the break from the world he undoubtedly deserved?

As if those upcoming occurrences weren't enough to wake me early, I was looking forward to my visit to the Buddhist temple. It was so striking and intimidating. I was thrilled to have the chance to visit it in real life and walk around the buildings and grounds. To feel what it felt like there. Again, with the pieces falling perfectly in place, when I looked up the

Watt Munisotaram, there was an announcement for its "largest summer event" coming up in just a few weeks. It promised cultural entertainment and food, as well as boasting to be kid-friendly. I couldn't wait to attend.

And I hadn't forgotten about Steven. I vowed to visit his grave once spring arrived. Craig asked me what I was hoping to gain by visiting. I shook my head without meaning to. "I'm not hoping to gain anything," I answered quickly. "I want to pay my respects. To say goodbye. To acknowledge his gift. Just to say hi."

But the cherry on top of my spiritual sundae was that Aileen, the past life regressionist, agreed to conduct a private group past life regression at my home, allowing the opportunity for me to have a final glimpse into the spirit world, seeing it with the mind that has learned and grown so very much. I felt elated and free, like I had just won a raffle or snagged the front parking spot at the school pick-up line. Additionally, Craig agreed to try a past life regression with us, after three years of being uninterested. My journey would come full circle, beginning and ending with a glimpse into the glowing energy field I'd seen four other times. I realized I sounded a bit like a junkie, jonesing for my next hit (or that could have been the four weeks without carbs talking), but seeing was believing. And seeing (experiencing?) that place was what led the charge to learn more. It was the beginning for me. And now it could also be an ending.

Walking in Memphis

IN BRIGHT AND cheery May, Paul Simon serenaded me mentally for days. You know, cuz I was goin' to Graceland. I had to explain what Graceland was to the kids after listening to the song several times.

"You will meet Elvis?" my daughter asked.

"No, honey. Elvis is dead. But he has a huge mansion that people go to see."

"Because he was rich?" she asked.

"Well, yes. And because so many people want to know more about him because he's such a famous musician."

She thought a moment. "Will you bring me a jewel?"

"What?"

"A jewel from Elvis. Since he was so rich," she clarified.

I laughed. "Maybe I'll find a necklace or something."

She seemed satisfied. Then threw me a curveball. "I wonder what a dead person looks like."

"Oh... Well, when someone we know passes away, we will go to a funeral and you can see. But they really just look like a sleeping person."

Her brow furrowed. "But I thought all the color left out," she said, making a motion of something coming out of her chest and floating away. "Aren't they gray? I thought all the colors left." She continued before I could reply. "Maybe a soul isn't a glowing ball like you think. Maybe it's a paint splatter of colors, Mom. Oh! Maybe you could write a book about that idea I just had."

"I was just thinking that!" I told her, having just finalized the book cover idea utilizing splatters of color. "But no, people are not gray when they are dead," I replied. We were silent a moment. "You're a pretty smart six-year-old," I said.

"I know," she said back. (Well, at least *she* trusted herself.)

While headed to Memphis, our plane hit turbulence as it split through a cloud. It made me slap Craig's upper arm from across the aisle. (I had ignored the email asking me to check in for our flight a few days prior, and no seats were left together.) I reminded him that our daughter had asked for a picture of what it looked like in the sky; what clouds looked like from up in the air.

As he snapped the image, I thought back to when I was a young girl, curious about the sky. In elementary school, when we had learned about the layers of the atmosphere from Earth to outer space, I had been perplexed. I remember bringing the paper handout home to ask my dad about it. My dad knew the answer to everything, it seemed. I brought it into my dad's home office and pointed to the layers drawn around the Earth. "But, Dad," I whined, frustrated I didn't know the answer. "If this is all the layers... then where does Heaven fit?"

Dad shook his head and smirked, saying something like, "That's a big question for such a little girl." He didn't give me an answer or explanation, which was completely out of character. It was a poignant moment in my development. For a while, I went around thinking I had stumped my all-knowing father.

But I now know that he likely had an answer, but it was too complex for a first grader to comprehend.

Thinking back to Melissa Divine's comparison to cogs in a clock, I looked around the plane. Hundreds of life stories filled the plane, yet all of them coincided at this point. In all of our stories—all of our clocks—going to Memphis in May was our shared life moment.

Craig handed me my small box of chicken pieces from across the aisle. (Yes, we were those people eating dinner and wafting crispy chicken smells through the plane at lunch time. Sorry, people.) I took a piece of chicken—no fries, no sauce. I was still learning how to eat low carb on the go—and we shared a cold brew coffee, passing it back and forth through the aisle in the sky.

Thanks to turbulence, the chicken and coffee churned and jostled enough that nausea caused me to close my eyes. In my semi-meditative state, I imagined finding Sweet Bea's name.

I was more afraid to find it than not. Because I couldn't trust myself, I suppose. What if I walked into the Civil Rights Museum and found a Beatrice Palmer? Would that convince me? Would I be able to "just trust" like Melissa Divine suggested?

My guess was no. But I wasn't sure why. Why was it so difficult to just believe?

I knew the odds were that I wouldn't find evidence of Sweet Bea. But would I see a familiar Baptist church? Or part of town that mirrored the images I'd seen? And if I did, would that just be my mind making sense of the chaos again?

Since I was still very unsure what I thought about my past life experiences, when I came across a comment in a metaphysical group about the lives being messages from the person's subconscious, I was instantly interested.

Someone posed a question to the group asking if fears in the current life were scars from a past life. It made me think of Vinny, my skyscraper builder from the 1920s.

You see, I have never been afraid of heights. Sure, there is a long list of other things that make panic creep up my throat like acid and my palms become sticky, but give me *humanity's most popular phobia*, and I just don't react.

I remember jumping off a roof into a snowbank without reservations as a kid, which everyone thought was out of character for a cautious individual such as myself. But with heights being no problem, why would elevators make me nervous? For as long as I could remember, I got overheated from the inside out and fidgety as I entered an elevator. Every noise got a thorough mental interrogation to determine just what had caused it. I looked at the ceiling of every one to see where that famed trap door was, to get out into the open shaft. But why the elevator uneasiness?

I made a note to ask Dr. Parrino the neurologist his perspective, but assumed I already knew the school of thought. The conventional thought would be that a fear of elevators crept into a dreamlike story I had told myself.

But the unconventional thought would say that because Vinny died in an elevator shaft, I somehow carried that with me; therefore I was afraid of elevators in subsequent lives.

I did not reply to the social media thread. But amid the replies from the group, many, many agreed that phobias were scars from a past life.

The opposing opinion was from a man from Seattle who was a private investigator and hypnotherapist—an appealing combination if I had ever heard one. He stated that during his schooling to become a Past Life Regressionist (PLR), he was taught that the messages were not from past lives or alternate realities, but rather from our own subconscious.

Yes. Just the thought I kept clinging to. Messages from the deep, dark untouched portion of our brain. That concept was easier for me to accept.

Though I hadn't planned to include another hypnotherapist in my interviews, I sent him my request, and he accepted within the hour. We made plans to connect after I was back in Minnesota.

Our visit to Memphis made an impact, alright. There for a three-day music festival, it was an accidental culmination of so many of the topics I'd written about before arriving. Music as a link to the spiritual world was all around us—especially at night, under the stars, in a sea of people all swaying and swelling with joy and excitement, all there to enjoy the same pattern of sounds from the same people on stage. It was enough to make me ask Craig if we should get matching, swirling tattoos to commemorate the experience. (We did not.)

But more than the music, there was the city. I went in wondering if Memphis would feel familiar. It didn't. I wondered if I'd find evidence of Sweet Bea. I didn't. But what I found instead was so compelling that if I close my eyes, I can still *feel*.

Memphis had a heartbeat. Memphis had a soul. Memphis was alive.

As we were there with friends from the area, we got to see all of the tourist stops. I was beyond thrilled to visit both Graceland and Sun Studio. But our first stop was to the Civil

Rights Museum. Summed up in a word? Solemn. So damn solemn. Tears threatened to drip from my eyes twice before I made it through. At one point, I was staring at a recreated silver streamlined bus, just as I'd viewed in Sweet Bea's life. When I mentioned the gleaming bus I saw rolling into Memphis during my past life regression, people assumed Martin Luther King, Jr. or maybe Elvis. But I had somehow known Sweet Bea hadn't been around for either of those occasions. When I saw the exhibit about the Freedom Riders, stared into the headlights of that shining, gray bus... it didn't seem wrong. And I lingered a long time, thinking about the courage and moxie those riders had possessed. Hoping if I *had* been Sweet Bea, I would have felt proud and excited to watch them roll into Memphis.

Just past the Freedom Riders, we entered a room dedicated to the songs and lyrics of the movement. We entered the room with a few women older than us. They began singing the songs along with the display. They knew the words without reading them. Yet, I had never heard a one.

Solemn.

We drove directly from the museum through the drizzling haze to Graceland, hopeful it would lighten the mood.

It didn't.

The rain that prompted us to spend twenty-six dollars on an Elvis umbrella didn't let up as we waited in line. And going through the mansion and hearing the stories—being reminded he was only forty-two, and then ending the tour at his actual grave on a dreary, spring morning? It was somber. Solemn and somber was our tourist day in Memphis.

So when we went to check out the pyramid the next day, I was happy to have something on the agenda with no mental heft. The pyramid in Memphis, which stands thirty-two stories tall, is home to a retail outlet. As we entered, our friends made a big deal about the elevator. As we entered, I understood why.

As the sign stated, we were looking at the tallest free-standing elevator in the United States.

Elevator. You see the irony, I'm sure.

I went to Memphis looking for a link to Sweet Bea, and instead found myself pondering the past life vision of Vinny. Sightseeing at a pyramid that housed an elevator was not something I had foreseen.

As the tallest free-standing elevator, there was (of course) a fee to ride it to the top. I prepared for the nervous feeling. I fully expected it. We paid our tourist fee and walked in.

But instead of creeping panic, being able to see the steel beams through the glass walls of the elevator all the way up made it seem more comfortable. I had no response at all, in fact. But I didn't understand why.

Once at the top, we stepped outside and onto a glass floor. I'll admit, I went out slowly at first, but then, I quite liked being able to see in every direction around me. Blue skies above, green grass below, the Mississippi River to my right and the city to my left. I leaned on the rail and let the wind blow my hair as I surveyed everything (noticing how many people were refusing to walk on the glass-bottomed balcony). I could see the musical festival stage from our vantage point. I took a moment to appreciate the fact that I'd grown up with the Mississippi River in my backyard and was looking at a whole other end of it; connected somehow. Linked.

Too soon it was time to head home. I tried to keep an eye out for the Baptist church I'd seen in my Sweet Bea experience, but there wasn't a lot of opportunity to drive around. We did pass a church that made me look twice—it was an old church, in bricks of white or beige with tall, arched windows. It was similar. An internet search concluded there were only three Baptist churches with that appearance. Maybe somewhere church records existed for a Bea Palmer, but after an hour of searching, I wasn't able to find them.

I put the idea to rest. For the remainder of the trip, we focused on the music.

Directly after Memphis (as in, the next morning after our returning flight), Craig was scheduled to go in for an outpatient surgery. While he was laid up and healing, I moved the television into the spare bedroom for him. He moved into the upstairs room while I slept downstairs with the kids. It was that perfect snippet of time in the year; windows open, tree branches swaying and brushing against the house, birds singing back and forth to one another, no frost in sight.

We opened the window next to the bed and curled up to watch the 1980s movie *Altered States*, as Jon from the Float Center had suggested. An hour and forty-four minutes later... I had no idea what we'd just watched. Craig declared it the "dumbest movie" he'd ever watched, though he didn't grow up a cinephile and was on pain meds at the time, still healing post-op. I thought it may have been one of the most bizarre movies I'd ever seen, but I wasn't even sure of that. I spent most of the movie trying to figure out what the message was. A man who physically went interdimensional through drugs and meditation and emerged as a caveman? Was that all it was trying to convey? Sadly, it was only somewhat coherent, and dreadfully trippy. But I did see how it would have been impactful to a young mind. And how it introduced sensory deprivation tanks, like Jon had said.

I emailed Jon and Melissa Divine to tell them we'd watched it and set up a time and date for the big day—the reading plus tank experience. But sadly, Craig's doctor said he needed to wait several weeks before he was able to float in a bath or pool (i.e., tank filled with magnesium sulfate). We agreed to reconnect in June.

Next, I contacted Aileen—thrilled to have a group past life regression right in our own house. But again, my message was met with disappointing news.

Aileen was in her last year of graduate school, planning to become a psychologist. This included a counseling practicum at a psychologist's office. Though she had not facilitated any past life regressions (PLRs) during the month of being there, her practicum supervisor found out that she was planning to facilitate PLRs. Abruptly, she was told she had violated the agreement and the site terminated her practicum. I was shocked! I knew a line existed between clinical psychology and fringe psychology, but Aileen had not even facilitated any during her time at the practicum site. It was an important reminder that I was writing about a somewhat taboo topic. My journey was not one accepted by the mainstream, for the most part. Consequences still persisted for those who attempted to toe the line.

With great disappointment, Aileen sent her regrets and had to cancel my private group session. After her practicum was terminated, she had to go in front of the counseling and psychological services department to explain the situation. The head of the department agreed with the site's decision and gave her a warning that she could not practice hypnotherapy while in the program—even though in the state of Minnesota, a license is not required to perform hypnotherapy or PLRs.

It had a happy ending for Aileen, though, who quickly found a new site for her practicum. She still planned to graduate in December. But it left me without a conclusive ending to the journey.

Aileen recommended a different PLR facilitator who was located about a hundred miles away, but I was hesitant to contact him. I had only ever used Aileen as my facilitator and I worried I wouldn't have a similar experience with someone new. But it did seem a reasonable decision, especially to see if I would experience a "life" with as much emotion and detail as I had with Aileen.

I reached out to him and began orchestrating plans with a Spirituality Center at a motherhouse of the Sisters of St. Francis, who had founded a prominent hospital in the area. I collected dates and mediated schedules to come up with a final date, time and location for the group session. Though I had imagined six of us splayed out on mats in my downstairs, instead the group had grown to fifteen, and the room was rented in an enormous religious building that still actively housed somewhere around a hundred Sisters.

The residual remnants of my Catholic guilt bubbled upward at the thought of hosting a workshop on reincarnation in a religious nunnery, but the rental contract said it was an open space for use for any type of spiritual endeavor. And this, most certainly, was that.

Visakha Puja

The Buddhist Festival

CRAIG AND I celebrated our actual anniversary at the end of May with a local wine tour by trolley. It was more than a month after his surgery, so he was able to participate. We met friends and enjoyed the sunny afternoon. I told them about my plan to host a group past life regression and they were interested. Soon after, our daughter graduated from kindergarten, successfully marking the completion of our first school year as parents. The following weekend was Visakha Puja—a holiday celebrating the birth, enlightenment and death of the Buddha—at the Buddhist Temple.

It was a perfect day for an outdoor festival, the end of May when every Midwesterner clamored to be outside and enjoy the mild, sunny days. Our GPS said the temple was just outside of Hampton, Minnesota—a town of 689 people.

We turned off the highway and onto a more local road. Along the winding drive, we passed an old Catholic church, a sportsman's club and an enormous wooden statue of a Minnesota Viking. In sum, very *rural Minnesota*.

The view from the road changed back into intermittent clumps of trees and cornfields before being closed in tighter by the woods.

Then, they appeared. Three steeples of gold. Wat Munisotaram, the Cambodian Buddhist Temple. We arrived at the entrance, lined with flags, along with a stream of cars. It seemed to be a popular and well-attended event... and we were late.

We followed the flow of traffic past brilliant buildings of red and gold, lined with intricate, carved railings and outbuildings filled with statues. But just as we arrived at the gravel parking area, a local police officer motioned for us to stop and roll down our window. "Looks like you get a front row seat to the parade," she said in her *Fargo*-thick accent.

The music and chanting propelled in through the rolled-down window. A sea of monks in orange robes followed a decorated truck, a majority carrying striped flags (and wearing white tube socks with sandals, which I found curious). On the back of the truck was a leader, chanting words in Cambodian into a crackling PA system. The trail of hundreds of monks chanted back in turn. They provided a dramatic contrast to the pale blue sky and puffy white clouds.

Craig looked down the pathway from where they were marching, then threw me a look. "We're going to be sitting here forever," he muttered.

We set the children free from their car seats to stand and watch the parade from inside the car. It was more of a march than a parade, though. Clearly symbolic. A greater part of the onlookers were families dressed in their Sunday best (Christian turn of phrase intended), picnicking in the grass and sitting together at wooden tables.

I noticed right away that no one seemed to be speaking English, which posed an issue as I am unable to speak Cambodian. "I wish I knew what was going on," I told Craig, craning to see past his head as the one and only "float" drove by.

"Is that a chicken seahorse?" our son asked, pointing to the gold statue's float that rivaled a Macy's Day Parade blowup in size.

"Look! There's a man riding the golden chicken seahorse!" our daughter chimed in.

Craig laughed; I tried to refrain. "I'm not sure, but I think that's an important symbol. We should be respectful and not talk like that."

The kids side-eyed each other in the backseat and dove tiny hands in for another handful of car-crackers (you know, the crackers that are purchased for the sole purpose of remaining in the backseat of the car). There we sat in the running car, with a line of cars idling behind us.

After several minutes, hundreds of ladies in long white dresses, carrying flowers, were flowing in a line in front of us.

Half a bag of car crackers later, the policewoman came back to our window. "Should be all right to go when the last of the parade passes... or maybe they don't call it a parade?" she asked, her hand on our open window.

Craig and I shrugged. We all exchanged awkward smiles and she walked away. I felt uncultured and uncomfortable for not knowing. But how better to learn?

We pulled into a parking spot and finally climbed out of the car.

"Ooh! I want to go see the water!" our daughter sang out, pointing to a large statue on a square of crystal water. A bridge led across the water feature to the statue at the center.

We headed over, passing swarms of people. Still, no one was speaking a word I could understand. We passed booths of food and trinkets for sale, water coolers and huge signs... everything was in Cambodian.

I squeezed Craig's upper arm. "Thanks for doing these crazy things with me."

He just smiled as we approached the bridge.

"I want a picture with the gold snake!" our son yelled, pointing to a snake statue at the start of the bridge with five, evil-looking heads. I realized the snake's body slithered all the way around the length of the platform. We snapped our photo; him in his Captain America baseball cap, the snake with its ancient, toothy glare. The drastic contrast made for a strange photo.

When we got to the end of the outcropping, to the statue at the center of the water, there was finally a sign in English. I pushed ahead a bit, eager to know what it said. *Remove shoes and hats.* Oh.

We opted to turn back instead. There was a young family taking a group photo in front of the carved statue.

On we went to the next section of the property—a temple half-constructed. It was guarded by statues of snarling lions (another requested photo stop). From there, we crossed over a walkway with multi-colored bricks that made patterns of stars and squares under our feet. Following the patterns led us up a staircase and to one of the temples with a golden steeple we'd spied from the road. It was surrounded by a half-wall of light-hued stones and painted flower petals in bright bubblegum-pink. When we wound around the ramps (all carved and colored and oh-so-detailed), we got to the main door only to realize inside was a group engrossed in prayer or meditation. We did not interrupt. In the background, the ceremonial parade was still progressing around the perimeter of the forty-acre property. Their chants echoed through the property, bouncing off the golden walls of the surrounding temples.

"I'm sorry if it's weird, but if I hear anyone speaking English, I'm going to stop them to see if they'll explain what's happening," I told Craig as we continued wandering the grounds.

He nodded in understanding as we came to another prayer area, this time encasing a Buddha that I recognized.

"Can we take our shoes off and go up?" our daughter asked, squinting in the sunshine, pointing to the sign.

"Sure," I said, slipping off my sandals and nudging them over to the preexisting pile of shoes in front of the stairs.

We went into the open-air temple area. We got there at the same time as a group of other lost-looking tourists. I was just about to ask them if they understood the meaning behind the ceremonies and prayers taking place around us, but as I approached, I heard a similar conversation between them. "I guess we have to take off our shoes," one grumbled. "The flyer said food trucks and live music," the other replied, shaking her head.

I opted not to start a chat.

Instead, I stared at the golden Buddha belly before me, curious if it was taboo to rub it. Again, I opted not to.

About ready to go, we followed a stone path under fragrant, flowering trees out to the farthest outdoor prayer area, which looked like a gazebo with a sculpture inside.

"Look at all the fluffalions!" our son proclaimed, plucking a white dandelion and blowing the seeds in the warm breeze.

We chuckled. "If only he realized the fluffalions were the reason he's been sneezing all day," Craig said, taking my hand in his.

When we reached the gazebo, we gazed at the stone statue inside. This one sat in the lotus yoga pose. It wasn't clear to me whether it was meant to be a man or a woman. I liked its ambiguity. Free to be.

On its upward-facing palms was a carved spiral; beginning at the center of the palm and circling outward, stopping just before the thumb. Below the hands was a donation box. I dropped in some money, prompting an argument from the kids because they, too, wanted to drop money into the wooden chest. I looked at Craig. "Out of cash," he muttered, leading us back up the stone path.

Just as we were about to walk back to the car, I overheard a group of teenagers talking about how boring it was to be waiting all day for their families. They were taking selfies in front of the buildings in provocative poses. Not very befitting of the sacred tone of the rest of the festival. Again, I opted not to start up a conversation. It seemed that to them, this was just a lame summer activity forced upon them by their parents.

On our way back across the grounds (stopped once again by the never-ceasing ceremonial march of monks and ladies in white), I saw a billboard filled with colorful images and words. It said in bold blue lettering: *Vasakha Puja commemorates the Birth, Enlightenment (Buddhahood), and Parinirvāna of Buddha.*

I found a sign I could understand!

I snapped a photo, then hopped on my phone. Parinirvāna was more than just death. It was a celebration of the release from cyclical existence, karma and rebirth. It was the real ending. The boss level. The ultimate goal, right?

I wanted to do a fist pump for Buddha. He did it. And maybe I didn't need to understand a word around me to be happy about that. If a cyclical existence was real, there was an ending. Perhaps a rare-to-experience ending, but an ending nonetheless.

Then, since we were in the midst of quintessential Minnesota, we took the opportunity to stop at a local ice cream shop before heading home. I cheated the diet and shared a drippy cone of goodness with Craig. I told him we were celebrating. For Buddha.

Three nights after the festival, I received a life-quaking email at around 8:00pm. I was carrying a bottle of wine and two glasses; Craig, a cutting board of cheese and olives. He was lamenting that he was lacking something in life, needing an outlet or group or project. We were casually brainstorming ideas for him when I noticed my phone notification flashing.

"I'm just not sure what I want to do next," Craig declared.

"What the heck!" I blurted.

"What?"

"What does this mean?" I yelped, holding my phone up for Craig to read. It was a two-sentence email from one of the editors of a longtime freelance gig of mine. The email said, "Would you be interested in taking over the magazine? I need to transition out."

His forehead crumpled a bit.

"I'm sorry!" I jumped in, dropping my phone and putting my hand on his shoulder. "We were just talking about you, and this is... really bad timing... but does that mean what I think it means?" I asked again, pointing to the words on the screen, still illuminated.

Craig took a drink from his wine glass. "I think so. You should email her back."

I did. We spent the rest of the night speculating and pondering what a switch like that would mean in our lives. If it was something I'd be good at, enjoy, succeed in. If it was even doable.

That night, I couldn't help but lie awake and obsess about the "ask, believe, receive" prophecy. I had asked out loud at the Jack Canfield seminar for an opportunity, specifically one that would allow me to organize women and caregivers—the magazine was specific to this demographic—and then I received it. What a synchronicity... What a decision.

It just doesn't matter

The Private Investigator Hypnotherapist

I N THE EARLY heat of June, I was inundated with messages wishing *Eid Mubarak* across all social media channels. I knew a little about the end of Ramadan for those practicing the Muslim faith, but not as much as I felt I should. I reached out to a friend who was a first-generation US-born citizen of Egyptian descent. Eid is a celebration marking the end of the month-long daytime fast for Muslims. After just three days of OMAD (one meal a day) fasting, I couldn't imagine going one month like that. I sent my friend a random soul email. He replied with a link to a local Muslim community group. After sending out a few questions, I spent some of the day reading about the Islamic faith.

According to one source, there were around 1.6 billion Muslims (compared to around 1.15 billion Hindus and around 2.2 billion Christians) in the world. In general, the Islamic view was that humans do, indeed, have a soul. And when the body dies, *Malak al-Maut* comes as a grim-reaper-type to take out the soul. Good behavior earned you an easy, comfortable soul extraction, but for those who have strayed? Not painless. (Eek. What an image.)

After some internet searching, I discovered that Muslims have a place after death called *Barzakh*, which was an interim "waiting room" between death and rebirth on judgment day. They didn't believe a soul ever died, but were clearly anti-reincarnation. (As a Muslim, believing in reincarnation would result in that painful soul extraction mentioned, which explained my friend's prompt declination to my earlier invitation to the group past life regression.)

Three days after Eid, I had my interview with the hypnotherapist/private investigator I'd discovered before Memphis. His opening background statement, once we connected via video chat, was, "I was in the military in intelligence and counter terrorism. We were tracking terrorists—religious extremists."

Richard Benack is both a hypnotherapist and licensed Private Investigator (PI) in the state of Washington. His companies, HiPerformance Security and HiPerformance Hypnosis, are successful, he believes, because of his strong background in the psychology of how people think. As a PI, Richard focused on intelligence gathering and computer forensics. (Far less man-with-cloak-and-magnifying-glass than I imagined when first reading about the career.)

Richard continued, "I was an Air Force Intelligence Officer—active and reserve—for twenty-two years. I worked on cyber-investigations, including analyzing captured terrorist computer systems and monitoring terrorist online activities. I also did similar work for tech companies tracking cybercriminals and extremists who might pose a threat to customers."

"That seems a drastic difference from hypnotherapy. What led you to become a registered hypnotherapist?" I asked the man through the computer screen.

He was in an office, in front of a window showing off a

lush array of Washington state's foliage. "Well, I was born Catholic—I mean twelve years of Catholic education—but I'm not practicing any longer. The Catholic Church trained me very well to think. I got a Minor in Religious Studies."

I mused to myself that I had stumbled upon so many strangers to interview who had prior schooling in religious themes. Not something I had expected to encounter as that wasn't a criterion as I sought interviewees. Did it go hand-in-hand that if you wanted to talk about the soul, you were more likely to run into people with schooling in religious themes?

"I was trained in hypnotherapy by The Wellness Institute in Issaquah. I also received my Master Neuro-linguistic Programming Training and Timeline Training in Washington." Richard stated, "For those who don't know, neuro-linguistic programming, or NLP, is a psychological approach involving communication for personal development or reaching personal goals. As an approach therapists can use, Timeline Therapy is a tool to make changes in peoples' lives. The theory behind this type of coaching is that events and habits are stored within certain times within our memories and subconscious, and by accessing them, they can be shifted or 're-imprinted' to move past a trauma or limit."

I nodded. "I wasn't aware of this type of approach, though it sounds similar to cognitive behavioral therapy, which is often used to alleviate symptoms of insomnia."

"Similar," he agreed. "Because of my work, I was often faced with the unpleasant. I faced instances of trauma and abuse. Past Life Regression (PLR) is just one of the therapy tools for dealing with issues the subconscious is not ready to work with directly. This way you get 'a person who is like me, but who is not me' i.e., a past life," he stated with air quotes. "This person in a 'past life' has the same issues as me and was able to deal with the same problems by..." He trailed off, rolling his hand in a gesture that meant "fill in the phobia or issue here." He summed, "PLR can be considered a metaphor by people who don't want to believe in past lives. But really, it just doesn't matter if it's a metaphor or not, because the message is where the healing comes from."

"So you do believe that regardless of where the message originated, the point should be processed by the person experiencing it?"

"Definitely," Richard agreed. "Coming from my perspective, when doing counterterrorism, I saw how religion and any ideology could be warped by people with malicious intent... the possibility to go from warped to violent. It took a profound toll on me and others. I worked with counselors. I wondered how *I* could help people? How did healing work? After seeing examples of intergenerational trauma, I became more sensitive to it. I understood how valuable and important it was to invest in mental health. It changed me, and how I relate to people."

"I can't imagine..." I muttered, the empath within squirming at the thought.

"Trauma is so deep," he continued, "that I believe it starts in the subconscious or soul. Real or metaphor, I don't know, but I know it's the place to start."

"So you don't feel the need to find out if past lives are real?" I asked, longing for that actual *Que Sera Sera* sense of being.

"Some people believe they are very real. Were they really Cleopatra? I don't know. They perceive themselves as that, so that's what I work with. It helps people heal whether it's real or not. It shows a pattern in life that can be used in healing."

"Have you ever seen any of your own past lives?"

"Yes," he answered easily. "Somewhere around nine to

twelve of them. I always seem to be some variation of a solider—World War II, Civil War, one version in 600 AD when I was a farmer who became a solider when my family was killed by bandits. But that all makes sense coming from my military background."

"Some of those sound specific. Have you ever tried to PI your own lives?" I asked, thrilled at the idea of a past life *missing persons* search that ended with details.

But instead, I got the same humorless look as when I'd asked Aileen about the psychic knowing I'd be contacting her. Deadpan. "No, I have never investigated. I just use them to discover how it can help with my healing."

I felt a bit like Rodney Dangerfield tugging at a tight collar before declaring, "Sheesh, is it hot in here or is it just me?" I moved on to the next question. "So what would you say your personal belief surrounding reincarnation would be then?"

"I guess I lean toward reincarnation. What that entails, I do not know. I don't have that insight."

I nodded. "And are you afraid of death?"

"Not really, no," Richard answered. "When I was younger, I was drawn to high-risk activities like sky diving, scuba and tough martial arts. But as I've gotten older and wiser, I don't go looking for those opportunities."

"Thoughts on the universe sending us signs or signals?"

"Signs?" He asked aloud, thinking a moment. "I think so. I mean, even if there was a sign, there would still need to be work involved. I don't believe the universe just *does* the work for us. But yes, I think signs are there..." After a moment, he continued. "Life is a powerful experience. Each person is on their own journey. Each person must decide what that is."

I was nodding in agreement, marking yet another interview that had looped back around to human experiences. "Well, thank you for your time, Richard. Those were all of my questions, unless you had anything else to add."

"Actually, yes. One thing that may be of interest. I work with a unique group in the area doing invocation trance work. It's best described like when someone says, 'he is really in the zone.' We work with weapons while in a heavily invoked—trance—state. Since beginning, my whole perspective has changed. It has been very deep for me. I started to perceive the world differently. The last couple of years, I felt a sense of fear in the community, but hypnosis, meditation or trance-like states... it can help people... help us not let the fears drive our emotions or behavior; to slow down."

"Interesting. I've interviewed a couple others who participate in somewhat similar practices. Have you ever tried Qigong, or Kundalini yoga?"

"I have done both," Richard shared. "I currently include Qigong in my martial arts and workout training. I use it to integrate my breathing techniques into all aspects of my work. I also use it to help manage my emotional state."

I wondered aloud if it would be helpful to manage a stressed-out emotional state. Richard thought yes. And as for the timeline talk, he also recommended reading the book *Adventures With Time Lines*, for further detail. We thanked each other politely and ended the call.

Interested to learn more about the coaching methods Richard had mentioned, I searched for classes such as Advanced Timeline Training. I discovered a person could be certified by a group called Quantum Training Institute, located in Australia, after a two-day course that costs $550 to $730 to attend (apparently there are coupon codes). Just another fun fact to pull out when you hear someone is visiting Australia. You're welcome.

A few days later, I heard back from Bassem Fadlia, board member and treasurer of the Muslim Community Circle. He was kind enough to answer some of my questions to better understand the religion. He began with a basic definition.

"Islam is the faith. Muslim is an adjective for people or things belonging to the faith," Bassem stated.

"I didn't realize. I'm so glad I asked," I told him. "Do you celebrate Eid?"

"Eid, which is the day after Ramadan ends, is one of the two biggest holidays in Islam. We start the day with a morning congregational prayer and sermon. Spend most of the day visiting family and friends and doing fun activities like picnics and big dinners. In Muslim-majority countries, Eid is a three-to-five-day public holiday, but here we celebrate mostly just one day. Oh, and like most holidays in all faiths, a focus on foods and giving gifts has crept into tradition, too."

"Can you explain more about Ramadan?" I asked.

"Fasting the month of Ramadan is part of what we call the five pillars of Islam," Bassem explained. "The five pillars are declaration of faith, praying the five daily prayers, fasting Ramadan, giving a percentage of your wealth every year to charity, and pilgrimage to Mecca, if you can afford it. One can't claim to be a practicing Muslim without doing the five pillars," Bassem assured. "The month of Ramadan is a spiritual retreat for us. We abstain from eating, drinking, sexual relations and even bickering or arguing from sunrise to sunset throughout the month. It teaches us that if we can control these basic urges, then we are capable of controlling any other vice we may have. We taste the hunger that poor people taste to empathize with them more, and help them. We are commanded to pray extra nightly prayers, read more Quran and do more charity during this month."

"What do you wish people understood about the faith?"

Bassem collected his thoughts. "Misconceptions about Islam are so widespread and pervasive; I have had people argue with me that Muslims worship the moon—and then get angry and continue to argue when I tell them that we don't."

I shook my head in sympathy.

Bassem continued, "The main thing I see with the people attending our open houses is the amazement that they never realized how connected Islam is to Christianity and Judaism. The mainstream idea, at least around here, is that Islam is totally different and at odds with the Judeo-Christian traditions and morals that are familiar in this country. Muslims think otherwise. Islam teaches us that it is the newest and final version of the same faith from the same God of Christianity and Judaism. We are taught to follow the same commandments of being honest, not lying, not stealing, doing no harm, being kind to family and neighbors, helping the poor and the orphans and standing up against injustice—even if the perpetrator is more powerful or more connected to us than the victim. Islam instructs that a just war is permissible only in self-defense and should only be directed at combatants. Extremist groups who obviously defy these rules have been thoroughly and repeatedly condemned by mainstream Islamic scholars and the Muslim public."

"I appreciate the overview. And I appreciate you bringing up the extremist groups, as they are the ones we tend to see in the press."

"I would advise people to do their own research," Bassem stated. "Media can present out-of-context, half-verses from the

Quran to claim it is advocating awful things, but if you read the whole verse—and the verses around it—you will realize a completely different conclusion. Or if you do not wish to read, just talk to Muslims and hear their side before you make up your mind."

Bassem, also an IT professional and soccer coach, was headed to a game. We thanked each other and he led me to the Muslim Community Circle website to learn more about the group, which held regular open houses for people of other faiths to ask any questions about Islam. They also organized interfaith events with other churches and synagogues, as well as spoke at local schools and colleges and answer student questions. Like the other organizations I'd come across in my journey, I was impressed with all they were able to work for and accomplish.

A few days later, I got a text that said, "Whoa I have to be naked???" It was Craig. He had received an appointment confirmation email with instructions and details from The Float and Healing Center for his sensory deprivation tank experience.

"Um... I hope that isn't a deal breaker for you... I just confirmed your float with Jon," I texted Craig back.

"Lol no just weird," was his reply.

Among other things mentioned within the email, a pre- and post-float shower were built into the time allotment, and that Craig would be in the tank for an hour and a half. It sounded like a personal nightmare; all those instances of public vulnerability. I hoped Craig wouldn't see it as such. Craig also had to avoid caffeine, shaving, hair dyeing and new tattoos for the days before the float. Good thing we hadn't opted for that wild trip to the Memphis tattoo parlor.

Gratitude & gifts

THE NEXT DAY, our jam-packed June calendar said it was the day to visit Steven's grave. It was farther away than I had first thought, but the cemetery was on the way to a cave famous in the region that we'd been interested in visiting. Unfortunately, it was also the day I was scheduled to meet the magazine owner in person to talk about the details of her leaving the magazine. It would be tight.

The night before, Craig had suggested we look up exactly where the small cemetery was located, instead of just driving off in the morning. (Forever my rock.) It turned out the cemetery and the town near it have similar names, and I had been looking up the wrong place. So after winding through a variety of gravel roads (making Craig relieved we hadn't taken the family muscle car as first planned), we realized we no longer had working GPS. With neither of our phones giving us automated directions, we made it to the cave tour just in time. We became Minnesota State Park pass holders, sticking the 2019 sticker on our vehicle, along with the preexisting Minnesota Public Radio sticker, inadvertently branding our family as a "type."

After the little legs of our offspring walked the entire hour-long, underground tour, the group stopped next to an aqua-colored pool within the depths of the cave. It was eerie and stunning. Our gazes lingered while the tour guide spoke. Our forty-pound three-year-old was in my arms by then and he snuggled into my face and whispered, "That is amazing." And it truly was.

We emerged from the cave entrance, crossed a bridge and got back in the car. It was time for our stop to visit Steven's final resting place.

Navigating with only the gray lines on our offline smartphone maps, we worked our way through gravel roads and fields until we saw a white, arched, metal sign. "That's it!" I yelped, causing Craig to brake hard.

"Why are we stopping, Mama?" our daughter asked.

I turned from the front seat to look at her. "You can stay in the car, honey. I just want to stop by a grave of an old friend."

"We want to come!" our son whined from his car seat.

Craig shook his head. "Let's just all go."

He turned off the car and we all got unbuckled, entering a cricket-filled, high-grassed area before the archway. For some reason, my cell service came back to life. In pinged a message from the magazine editor canceling our meeting in a few hours. "Well, we don't need to hurry back," I told Craig.

The four of us walked in under the thin, metal arch—its white paint peeling off in flecks from the weather and years.

"What's the name, Mom? I can read the names," our daughter told us.

The look of adventure and excitement for the hunt made a weird grin come over me. As children, my siblings and I had held the same look when our father stopped at seemingly random cemeteries and sent us out to search for specific names on gravestones. He told us our help in finding the names filled in the gaps in our family tree (which he has mapped back to the 1600s). As an adult, I see he must have known exactly where to send us out looking. It was nice that he let us believe we were the brave explorers who had found the coveted, essential information.

I watched my young children dash from stone to stone, searching for Steven. But my eyes locked in on a stone in the farthest back corner. I headed that way and my family noticed.

"Did you find it?" she yelled, running with her brother ahead of me. "This says S-T-E-V-E-N," she spelled.

Craig came up and put a hand on each of their shoulders. "Let's let Mom have a moment alone, guys."

"No!" whined our son. "We want to see, too."

"It's okay," I told him. I saw my daughter's face scrunching up.

"I'm sorry your friend is dead, Mom," she said to me.

I sent her a sad smile of thanks and placed a small guitar-pick shaped stone on top of his grave. I was about to say my words, but the kids butted in once again. "I'm going to give him a fluffalion!" our son declared, picking the longest-stemmed one he could find.

"I'm going to give him this purple wildflower," our daughter said.

They placed their gifts at the top of the stone next to mine.

"Come on, guys. Let's go get some lunch," Craig interjected. "Maybe they will have grilled cheese at the restaurant."

"Yeah!" they called, racing back to the car.

I took my moment alone. I said my hello. My apology. My wishes for his peace. My goodbye.

Standing there... I didn't feel like he was there. But I didn't feel like he was *nothing*. I felt like he was somewhere. Which, I suppose, meant I was back to believing in a soul, one hundred percent. So far, my open-mindedness and readiness to adopt new belief systems had kept me afloat and curious, but being faced with a gravestone... Well, I wasn't ready to pronounce myself a nonbeliever.

After a minute of silence, I turned to leave, then looked back and said aloud, "And if the psychic mentions anything about visiting a friend's grave recently, I *will* freak out."

It was the first Tuesday of our new summer schedule when I received a strange phone call. My daughter was at a daytime summer camp and my son was at his first week of PreK. I was at work when I noticed a missed call from an unknown number. I'd been working with the rental person at the Spirituality Center for my group hypnotherapy session, so I assumed it was her calling me back with details.

But when I listened to the message, I didn't know what to think.

"Hello, this is Dee with the public school system. This call is in regards to your daughter. Please call us back before 4:00pm today," was the gist.

I was so confused. No one was at school. It was June. I dialed the number she had left and the call went a little something like this, "Hello, Ms. Dewink, did you put your daughter's name in for the elementary school lottery last year?"

"Yes..."

"Did you mark the box that you would be interested in other lottery school openings if they should become available?"

"Yes..."

"Your daughter's name was selected in the school lottery

system for the South Montessori School. Do you want the spot?"

I was dumbfounded. Shocked. "Can I have some time to talk it over with my family?"

"Yes, please call me back in one week at this number. Thank you!"

I had been told the lottery was over and there was a waiting list. I didn't know how another lottery was held to randomly select our daughter, but I was elated! I'd been putting her name in since she turned four.

My hands were shaking as I called Craig at work. I was searching for the school online at the same time.

The school was literally on the opposite side of the city, in a sketchy part of town.

The first thing Craig asked when I told him was, "How long of a bus ride would that be?"

I didn't know. And it was summer break. And I wasn't sure how to find out. Next, I called the Montessori school directly. I got the answering machine and the recording literally said, "We are closed for the summer. Do not leave us a message."

I started digging online, searching for any clues about the school. Craig reached out to parent friends in the area. Meanwhile, everyone we told congratulated us. Afterall, our daughter had just won the lottery.

Communicating
with the dead

ON A SUNNY Friday in June, we managed to coordinate my schedule, Craig's schedule, my cousin Becky's schedule and her daughter's schedule to babysit our children (as well as both Melissa's and Jon's) for the big day: the psychic reading and the float. Becky arrived at our house a few minutes late. In a rush, Craig and I said goodbye to the kids, tossing a brief overview to the sitter, and we all left in a hurry.

On the car ride over, I filled Becky in on some of the highlights I had already gleaned from Melissa and Jon, twisting back to chat with her while Craig drove downtown.

"I don't have any expectations," Becky said from the crumb-lined backseat. (Craig had remembered to remove the car seats; had not remembered to clean off the seats.)

"I don't either, but for some reason I've been nervous all week," I told her as we careened through a yellow light.

"I'm nervous too," Craig added. "Ninety minutes is a long time!"

"Yeah, it is," I agreed. "I couldn't do it." I smiled and squeezed his hand.

"Doesn't sound bad to me," Becky chimed in.

"I want to try it," Craig agreed. "Maybe I can get some answers to these big issues."

"That would be nice..." I agreed, still wondering if I would own a magazine soon, or if our daughter would begin first grade at a new school.

We pulled up to the blue house-turned-business three minutes before the appointment time. Melissa met us at the door and welcomed us all inside. Jon motioned for us all to come in and get comfortable.

Melissa was wearing a flowy, blue skirt and a dangling ball necklace that slid side-to-side along her collarbones as she walked. "Well, how would you like this all to start?" she asked me once we'd all been introduced.

"I was thinking Craig could get orientated and start first, then while he's floating, you could conduct the reading with Becky?"

Everyone agreed to the plan. Jon, who stood taller than my often-tallest-in-the-room Craig, handed out clipboards. "These are the intake forms I give all first-time clients," he explained. After receiving an overview on the float, Becky decided to also complete a form in case she came back to give it a try.

I snuck a peak at the form. It asked for personal details about health ailments, spots of pain in the body, a light outline of medical history, history of depression and anxiety. I looked to Jon, "Why do you need to know all of this for a float? Is it dangerous for some people?"

"No, not at all. That's my intake form for the Healing Center overall. I also do reiki work."

I nodded, looking over Becky's shoulder. "Wait, this form references *Altered States*?" I said with a laugh. I pointed to the spot on the form that assured floaters they would not be turned into an interdimensional ape-man during the process.

Jon chuckled. "I didn't even write that! It is standard template wording for floating."

Melissa smiled. "I guess now I have to watch this movie!"

Craig didn't even look up from his clipboard when he stated in a flat tone, "Don't."

Once they were all finished, the four of us went for the orientation about the tanks. Instead of entering the room with the familiar canvas picture, Jon led us downstairs. There was a larger room with space for us all to congregate around another large white tank.

"Floating is effortless and safe," Jon began. I could sense how pleased he was to share his passion with us. "Within the tank, there is just ten inches of water with 800 pounds of Epsom salt, magnesium sulfate. The water is set to a warm 94.5°F. Because the water is so salty, keep it away from your face," Jon warned. "In case it drips into your eyes, there is a spray bottle of fresh water and towel just outside the door to flush your eyes with." He looked to Craig and smiled. "I've done the research for you—the stinging subsides in about two minutes, but it's very different than having a drop of ocean in your eye," he chuckled. I looked to Craig, too. He seemed nervous.

Jon opened the large door of the tank and showed us the step and handrail. "Once you're in there, you'll want to try to clear your mind. Focus on your breath. Concentrate on the sensation of floating. You will be so buoyant—like a cork," he added, "that one tiny flick of a finger will send you drifting across the tank. It will feel like time has slowed. I like to count how long it takes to touch the other side. It's like drifting down a long hallway. Just picture where you want to be."

He closed the door and faced us. "Some people say things slow down so much they can feel their heartbeat... feel the blood flowing through their body."

"What if I get so relaxed that I fall asleep?" Craig asked.

Jon smiled a kind smile. "It's safe to sleep in there. I know I have. And only once out of many times, I turned my head to the side and got a bit in my eye. That woke me up!"

Craig visibly gulped. "I don't know if I can turn my brain off..."

Jon motioned for us all to head back upstairs as he spoke. "I know there can be a log jam of stuff in there, but it can clear up. Let's get you started upstairs. You can use the tank in the back room."

We all marched in a line up the staircase from the basement and Jon showed Craig the upstairs bathroom. "You'll find everything you need in here. After your shower, you can use that robe and head into the tank. I'll fade out the music after a few moments of you being in there. Feel free to turn off the light once you're settled. Happy floating!"

Craig gave me one last look and headed back behind a white curtain. I sent him my *good luck* face and turned back to the ladies.

"Well," Melissa started. "That leaves it to us."

Becky and I took seats on the long sectional; Melissa pulled an arm chair close to us. As she was sitting, she asked, "Have you ever had a reading before?"

"No," Becky replied. "Unless you count a palm reading in third grade."

We all chuckled. Melissa looked to Becky. "You may have noticed that I went downstairs with you," she began. "I wanted to stay with you the entire time. I wanted you to be sure that I had no chance to research you."

Becky shook her head; the thought never having occurred to her, being very open to the experience.

"I communicate with the spirit world," Melissa continued. "I also connect with energy—of you, your house, your mom, your sister—whatever. But that part is Earthbound. I access universal knowledge. If at any point you feel I am going too fast, or you need to pause—stop me. Or if we enter a point that is unclear, you can tell me. You can give me as much as you feel comfortable giving me. But we don't know each other," she pointed from herself to Becky and back. "We have never met."

Becky shook her head, agreeing. I heard Craig leave the bathroom behind us and enter the float room.

"I know nothing about you except that you're Gina's cousin."

We both nodded.

"Something to know about me, I will never let something *just fit*. I won't accept a *false yes*. I'll give you info from the spirit world that may come to me as pictures or symbols. It can be a bit like a game of spiritual Pictionary! We can work to figure it out. Your reading will be one hour long. We'll just see where things go. I let the spirits guide a reading rather than me. Does that all sound okay?"

"Yes," Becky said, her arms crossed around herself. There were a lot of instances of open vulnerability going on.

"Then let me just get ready," Melissa stated, moving her chair even closer to Becky. She perched herself cross-legged on the arm chair. "I just need to re-center myself... let go of my stress and ego..." she said while taking deep breaths. Her eyes closed and her blonde hair brushed her bare shoulders. She opened her eyes. A look of sympathy took over her face. "Right off the bat, I'm getting that the past six months have held a lot of upheaval and changes and scrutiny. You've been looking at things very carefully. It's sort of a 'once and for all! I am never going back to that!'" Melissa explained with enthusiasm.

I dared a peek at Becky. There were tears welling up in her eyes. It was apparent Melissa had nose-dived into an emotional well.

Our psychic medium continued. "You are not going back there," she stated in a sure tone, complete with a positive head bob. "You are not doing that again. It's been a quiet time, but tumultuous inside..." Melissa looked right into Becky's eyes. "Girl! You've been beating yourself up!"

Becky allowed the mass of tears to release with Melissa's words. The spheres of shimmering liquid streamed over flushed cheeks. I felt like an intrusion on a private moment. And I was stunned with the reaction, as we were only a few minutes in. I looked back to my notes, allowing Becky a bit more privacy in her moment.

"There has been a lot of damaging self-talk," Melissa said. She started going into details, all the while with me trying to sink under the couch cushions and give them space while simultaneously wondering how the words seemed to be straight out of Becky's mind. Melissa spoke about private thoughts and things happening in Becky's life. "But it's time to let it go," she coached. "Those tense energies... negative energies. Honestly, it would be a good thing to leave in the tank." She motioned toward the tank room behind us. "To visualize the water washing over and through and washing the toxins away. Creating new internal talk. Reprogramming and switching all that self-talk." She focused again. "We can talk more about how to do that afterwards if you want to."

Becky grabbed a tissue and nodded.

"Now your spirit guides... spirits here for your higher

good." She tilted her head to the side a bit. "Did you lose a parent... six or eight... six or eight months ago?"

"Seven years," Becky whispered.

"Years. I said months. It's been years," Melissa seemed to say to herself. "That seems to be a big part of what's been going on. The release and letting go. You said seven years, but it seems like something fresh... You keep regurgitating it..."

"Yes," Becky stated, looking so sad I wanted to hug her; feeling bad for making her go through this.

"It's your dad that's passed," Melissa said.

"Yes."

"When we were all standing in the basement, I felt a strong male presence. That was him. Your dad's energy blended with mine, and I started feeling hot and flushed from the intensity of his energy. It was so intense I had to remove my outer sweater! He was very excited to get the mediumship party started, to have his sentiments heard by you for the first time."

That made Becky smile. So far I didn't know what to think, but I knew enough about my uncle to know he was jolly and large and always overheated.

"I'm getting a sense of humor," Melissa started again. "Humor, wit and... playful? Your dad is coming though with a one-of-a-kind sense of humor."

Both Becky and I started to cry. Believe it or not, the number one thing people loved about Becky's father was his playful humor. They were the perfect words to describe him.

Melissa got serious. "It's... it's difficult for him to see you like this. Difficult to take the sidelines and watch you. Oh!" she interrupted herself. "He said, 'make sure she knows it's not really the sidelines.' He's here for you."

I swallowed, feeling the room take on a strange vibe. I told myself I was making it up in my head, but I was a little uncomfortable.

Melissa continued, "Tinker..." she mumbled. She made a squeezing motion with her hand. "He's showing me those things—what are those things?"

I looked to Becky. She was on the edge of her seat.

"Vice grips!" Melissa yelped. "Constant fixing, though things are never fully fixed. Vice grips are on, but nothing is ever... nothing is ever unbroken," she explained, seeming like she was engaged in a mental game of Pictionary. "It's hard for him to sit there and not get in there and tinker. He's heard you ask him for help. But then you put on the brakes and you don't allow help. He's acknowledging the conversations you've had with him. Feels like a metaphor—one foot on the brake, one on the gas. That's you." Melissa delved into more examples of the things Becky has needed help with. I didn't know if the details provided were true or accurate. I didn't know the deep secrets of my cousin-friend. Melissa ended that portion by declaring, "Things are changing! People will invite you and you will actually go. Miraculous things are opening up for you!"

Becky was grabbing another tissue as Melissa shook her head a little. "Dad says there are no shortcomings there where he is... and he's... obsessed with his hair?" she asked us with a quizzical look.

After a moment of silence, Becky offered, "I don't know that he was, but most of my life he didn't have any hair."

"Well he does now!" Melissa blurted, causing us both to smile. "He's showing off his jet-black hair... like tossing it dramatically in my face."

Neither Becky nor I chimed in to reassure Melissa; the truth being that his hair was never black, but the family was obsessed with Elvis. My uncle was the kind of guy to walk in a room wearing a silly wig, just to wait until we noticed so we could all share a laugh. And no matter if it was a real message from him or not, the joke still worked. Becky and I were both laughing through tears in our eyes at the image. I felt a little sorry for Melissa, who wasn't in on the joke.

Next, she merged into the topic of self-care and learning to accept help. She spoke about ways Becky could combat negativity. She reminded, "When you say things like, 'I got this. I'm independent. I don't want to bother people,' when you tell the spirits 'I don't need help,' they *have* to listen. But it's okay to ask for help. It's okay to accept it. Lean on others." She suddenly pointed right at me. "Lean on *her* because I have a feeling she can handle it."

It was a peculiar thing to be singled out by a medium allegedly communicating with spirits. I hunched down into my notepad, already on page five, appearing the part of a guilty voyeur just caught in the act. Melissa had asked me to keep time and I noted it was about half way through the hour.

"But you've survived a really long time like this..." Melissa stated, focused on Becky once again. "I don't know how she did it. That's what Dad says. And you appreciate how huge that is, don't you? He was the rock. For him to say it... Girl, you are *fierce*! Stop being so fierce!"

Out of character for my uncle to speak like that, but it seemed like that was just Melissa's interpretation of his message.

She continued, "Gentle up a bit. It's okay to soften now. Once you get that, you will be in a place of knowing and loving yourself..." Melissa made a weird smirk. "Okay, so we make new friends in Heaven. My uncle and your dad are laughing about their bellies now."

We both chuckled. I looked around the room, searching for any evidence that we weren't alone.

"But does all of that make sense? Is there anything else you want to know?" Melissa asked.

Becky spoke for the first time in a long time. "Is there an end in sight to how exhausted I am all the time?" she asked, her voice cracking from the weight of sincerity.

Melissa physically deflated with relief. Then she smiled a bright smile. "Yes. Your obligations are lessening."

Becky's tears flowed over her reddened complexion. Again,' I wanted to hug her.

Melissa gave special instructions and ideas as to how to welcome positive energy and assistance from others. Then she tilted her head to the right. "It seems there's a female presence. Spunky, respectful... quiet until you get to know her... quirky and odd. She is a maternal energy. She has strength of conviction. She has been standing behind you. Helping you stand upright. Her role is to be the backbone, but she's maternal. I see her rocking your children like babies... but they're not babies, are they?"

"No," Becky offered. "They are nineteen and sixteen."

"Really?" Melissa asked, momentarily snapping back to the room. Becky looked very young, on top of being young when she had children. It often caught people by surprise. "Well, I see her as strength and courage and spunk. The answer to prayers, offering levels of support. Shoring up your backbone. It could have been a dark route, but you championed it. She's commending you... for your strength of character. And she really wants you to know... she wants you to know it will *never* get this bad for you again."

Both of us let tears fall at her final words. What a powerful message. From the spirit world or from another human, what a glorious reassurance. I wanted the words to be true. I never wanted Becky to have to go through the darkest of times again.

Melissa went on, "It's like a hundred-year storm has passed... You're good. It's behind you... and you received a gift."

We both looked up.

"Your dad... so thoughtful. He could have just shown an image of a plain cardboard box, but he's handing you a perfectly wrapped box, the kind you can lift the cover off of and it's wrapped all the way around. It has holes in the cover. You've recently gotten a pet."

At that point, we both nodded profusely. "Yes, I just adopted a cat," Becky stated.

"And she's allergic to cats!" I couldn't help but blurt.

"But you're not allergic to this... to this angel." Melissa just seemed to know.

"I'm not." Becky's head was shaking in disbelief.

Melissa ran her hands up her arms. "I just got chills! It's so beautiful. She was your sign. Your rainbow after a long rain. A gift from your dad."

"I didn't think of it until right now!" Becky suddenly squeaked through tears. "When we were young, I had an outdoor cat named Mittens. She was hit by a car, but didn't die. My poor dad had to put her out of her misery. I knew he didn't want to do it!"

My hand was on my chest. I remembered that sad, grim, summer day from our youth as well.

"And the cat I just adopted... her name is Mittens!" Becky was sobbing harder than I'd witnessed in years. I could tell she had accepted it all as truth. She was a believer.

Melissa stood up from her chair. "I'm going to hug you," she said rather than asked. I was relieved *someone* was hugging her.

It had been torture for me to not comfort Becky through the emotional journey.

They hugged for a long time. A very long time. Melissa muttered, "You don't have to do it all" and "This hug is also from your dad" during the prolonged embrace.

And then... the room went back to normal. I know how that may sound, but it was almost like waking up from a dream. We heard Craig showering in the other room, already out of the tank. Jon came back up from downstairs.

Melissa said something to Jon and I took the opportunity to turn to Becky and whisper, "Did you feel like he was in the room for a moment there?"

"Yes!" she replied.

Melissa overheard. "*Definitely* in the room," she reassured.

"Now that the reading is over," I said to Melissa. "I'd love to tell you more about Becky's dad. He owned a bar, but never drank. He was jolly and friendly to everyone. He was a picker and a tinkerer."

"The vice grips!" Melissa chimed in.

"He was like a second father to Gina," Becky interjected. I was amused that we seemed to talk for each other.

I nodded in agreement. "I remember one time we went picking in an abandoned trailer. I found a ceramic jewelry holder shaped like an upturned palm—very swingin' sixties, hippie-looking—and he let me keep it. I put my rings it in every night and think of him almost every time my jewelry clinks the swirling ocean tones inside the hand."

"I don't remember that," Becky said to me.

"You went on so many junk picking adventures. I had fewer to remember."

Just then, Craig emerged from the back. All four of us turned to look at him. His eyes were so large they looked brown or black, even though their natural color was bright blue.

"How was it?" I asked, afraid I'd read on his face that it was awful.

"Enjoyable," he said. He walked slowly toward the couch. "I need to get my balance back though."

Jon smiled from his position next to Melissa in an arm chair. "It takes a bit."

Poor Becky was still cleaning up her face, seeming glad the focus was no longer on her.

"You were right about time slowing down," Craig said. "And it was hard to tell where I ended and the water began."

Jon was nodding knowingly.

"But I did get the water in my eyes when I sat up to turn off the light."

"Oh, no!" I blurted. "I've never seen your eyes look like that. They're not red though."

"Yeah, I got it out. It took a solid two minutes like you said," he told Jon. Then he looked at me. "I kept feeling like I wasn't doing it right. I did the finger flick thing... it was neat. And it was nice just to not be obligated to do anything... but it was also a little long."

"The calm can span over the next three or four days. You'll have that feeling of calm with you," Jon offered.

"Do you feel calm?" I asked.

"Yeah, I do... and a little seasick."

We chuckled and got ready to say our goodbyes. It had been a long and powerful evening. We hugged and said our thank yous and headed back to the car.

"I did come out with one answer," Craig said to me. "She needs to go to that school. It's what will be best for her."

I smiled, opening the passenger side door. "Well, that's

something, Mr. Indecisive. You came out with an answer!" I noticed Becky still using a tissue. "I sincerely hope that wasn't too terrible for you," I said her.

"No, it was one of the best moments of my life," she stated.

It was a thoughtful and quiet drive back through the city. We filled Craig in on a few of the details, but were mostly still.

As we were dropping Becky off at her house, she asked, "When you said you sensed Dad in the room... where was he?"

"Standing right next to her on the left," I answered.

She bobbed her head in a strong nod. "Me too."

Though I wished I had done it before the reading with Melissa Divine, I looked up the definitions of the words I had mixed up in my mind. From what I could find, even general definitions were up for debate. (And, I'd like to note, none of the descriptions I found mentioned an ability to predict the future, outing my joke about the psychic knowing I'd call before I called as ignorance.)

Medium

A person who communicates with the deceased; the liaison between the spiritual and physical world. Mediums receive information from spirits. Frame of reference also makes a difference in how different mediums perceive things. Spirits *and* psychic senses run through the filter of the medium's experiences, memories and beliefs.

(Meaning, you cannot remove the medium from this type of mediumship, known as Mental Mediumship, because the messages are run through the mind of the medium, and each will receive and perceive differently.)

Psychic

A person who is able to use extrasensory perception (sometimes called ESP) to distinguish information the five senses cannot detect, such as someone's internal thoughts and emotions. Psychics receive information from a "sixth sense" or by reading a soul or aura of a person.

Clairvoyant

A person who sees information intuitively using a "third eye." Though it is the most commonly used word for receiving this type of information, it is just one of many types of people who believe they receive intuitive messages. The others are CLAIRAUDIENCE: hearing intuitive information, CLAIRCOGNIZANCE: just knowing (gut instinct) intuitive information, and CLAIRSENTIENCE: sensing or feeling intuitive information.

I took time to reflect on the definitions. It was so far into the supernatural realm that I wondered how hard an eye roll it might receive from the Humanists or Atheists. I wondered what I thought about it all.

During my initial conversation with Melissa Divine, she had commented about me, words that had hung in the air. She mentioned my ability to take several parts and put them all together into something that was easy for people to understand. It was a strange thing to note, since that was literally in my job description, as well as something I often cited as a strength of mine.

Had she read my aura? Sensed my spirit? Known some of my inner thoughts?

I could have asked her.

But some things were better off as ponderances. Part of me was afraid she would tell me my ability to read people, experience "bad feelings," and know about things before they happened were some sort of skill I forgot to hone. A bit like if Wonder Woman was told at age thirty-seven surrounded by her three cars, two children and sweet husband, that she had always been a superhero, but had overlooked her powers until middle-of-life sag was ever present. (Not that I'm comparing myself to Wonder Woman... or implying her super body would be subject to sagging. Just an illustration.)

On the other hand, if it was all made up in my mind... well, if that wasn't just admitting to a touch of pronoia.

I emailed and asked the neurologist, Dr. Parrino, if he had any thoughts on the psychological delusion of pronoia. Specifically, I asked if for the people who believe the universe is sending signs or directions, could pronoia be a more clinical explanation?

His reply was poignant and poetic. He explained, "Positive thoughts can create positive emotions. However, childish optimism can easily shift into idiotic or unrealistic optimism or even Pollyanna syndrome, believing possible the creation of paradise on Earth. The universe is certainly sending signs and information, but these inputs have no ethical meaning because the laws of nature are non-ethical. Giordano Bruno was convinced of a dynamic and solid interaction between macro- and micro-world and was burnt alive in a famous Roman square (Campo dei Fieri). Perhaps, mathematics and physics can provide tools to partially capture this mysterious language."

Once more, I was reminded that I was lucky to be on such a search without great fear of loss—of rights or of life. But since I had his attention on my project once more, I also took the opportunity to ask his thoughts on the theory that a person's phobias could have been caused by trauma experienced in a past life.

Dr. Parrino replied, "Psychological wellness is generally based on positive memories. However, some people tend to overemphasize the negative experiences of their lives. Sometimes, the mental scars provoked by a traumatic event are really deep and do not disappear, perpetuating a vicious cycle in which everything goes wrong because everything has always gone wrong. If current misfortune is attributed to a trauma in a previous life, then we move to a realm of religion or deeper psychiatry."

I wondered if Dr. Parrino would feel the need to recommend a good psychiatrist after perusing the pages of the book in which he was quoted...

I also was reminded of Richard the hypnotherapist's main point: that it just doesn't matter if the visions were real lives or not, if the healing occurs. Maybe I just needed to accept without hosting another internal debate. Could I do that?

It had been exactly three weeks since my initial email from the magazine editor. She and I had tried and failed to meet in person four times. I was a wreck. My fingernails were chomped down to nubs, my hair was falling out, I wasn't sleeping... Stress, man.

I had consulted a financial advisor, a business owner, friends, family, editors and even a psychic, if you counted asking Melissa Divine what it was like to run her own business. And after wheeling around and around each and every day for three weeks, I was sick and needed to get off the ride. It was just too easy to see why it was both an amazing opportunity and something I would excel at, as well as an unsound decision for us. Being a writer for many local magazines, I had gone so far as to set them all in a row on the floor in my office, selecting the ones I thought had the best layout and design, structure and printing. I had the June issue from my hometown region's magazine at the front of the line, as the best design and layout of the lot. I'd done countless hours of research on the print business and management. But still I was unsure.

We had discovered more details about our daughter's school opportunity. The bus would take over an hour each way, with one or two transfers along the way at various church and school locations. If we stayed in our current home, she would be gone more hours in a weekday than I was. We wondered if it would all be worth it.

But then we saw it: a webpage devoted solely to the Montessori's art studio. And scrolling through the images made actual tears prickle my eyes. It was our daughter's dream program.

Since the age of one, our daughter had shown amazing artistic ability. As a toddler, she was doing watercolor paintings. By age two she was coloring as well as an elementary student. By four, five and six, she was drawing and creating at a level that rivaled my own. Her art bordered on a compulsion—she did not go a single day without creating something. And it looked like we were being offered up a new school that allowed amazing opportunities such as children's art to be hung in hospitals and entered as part of fashion shows and art gallery collections. It was a golden opportunity. And also something I had specifically asked the universe to send us.

It was serendipitous that she was drawn in the lottery for

the one and only school in our city that offered such an art program. We couldn't say no, despite the crazy bus schedule.

We started looking at moving to the other side of town. It would ease up the commute if I was driving her, or shorten the bus ride if I wasn't. We looked at it as an investment in our children, since our son would also be granted admission once he was of age. But even as we looked, I heard the saying "prepare your child for the path, not the path for your child" repeating in my head. I was unsure moving was something most people would consider.

With a hard peach pit of sadness in my stomach, I composed the email declining the magazine offer. The timing was just not right for our family. I said no to something I thought was a dream...

But dreams evolve. They change. They become less important with the promise of alternate bright futures.

And after I emailed my sad declination, I called the school system with our final decision to transfer our daughter to the Montessori. (It was a big day for life decisions.)

I'd love to say I felt lighter (and I physically did, since it was day one of my final three-day fast of the twelve-week program), but mostly I felt unsure. In fact, I would have asked for a sign to show me I was making the right decision... but at that point, I feared the universe viewed me as a spoiled brat—asking and receiving and then declining what was offered.

Later that day, after the dust from all of my big decisions had settled, the universe got in one final jab. As I checked in with my newly-reconnected second cousin, Michelle, to ask if she wanted moral support for the final fast, she replied that she was on a deadline and too stressed to participate. I asked what project she was working on, unsure of her career. She told me she was a graphic designer and photographer. When she told me about the project with the major deadline, I yelped out loud!

For she was the very designer of the regional magazine I had selected as the best design; the one I would have hunted for if the magazine deal had gone through; the layout designer of the magazine at the top of my pile. My talented, freelancing cousin, who could have helped make my magazine dreams come true. The dream I had declined earlier that same day.

Well played, universe. Well played.

What we experienced

The group past life regression

T HE WEEK BEFORE the group session was planned, Craig's vehicle took its final tank of gas before heading to that big parking lot in the sky. The kids were staying with my sister for a few days, and instead of the magic to-do list (you know, the secret one in your head of all the things you'll accomplish once the kids are away), we spent the week looking for a new vehicle. Though we had known it was a looming possibility since the gas tank fiasco at Target, searching for a car wasn't on the agenda. Too soon, the kids were back home and Craig still didn't have a vehicle.

That late June morning, Craig left early to car shop before our 10:00am past life regression was to begin. My sister and I dropped off the kids at the sitter's and drove the winding pathway that led up the hill to the spirituality center. It was a hot and humid Saturday. We arrived early to set up the room before the other attendees arrived.

A kind front desk lady with gray hair smiled and ushered us to the elevator that would take us to the basement level. I had signed the paper and sent in a deposit without ever having seen the rental space.

After taking an aged elevator down a floor, we emerged into a dimly lit hallway. To our left, a dead end. To our right, a corner. After rounding the corner, we were faced with a long, gray, dark hallway with no windows. My sister found a light switch and made overhead lights flicker back to life.

A few doors away was the lounge we had reserved. Inside, a pink-hued carpet centered the room, edged by vintage wicker furniture.

"Oh, it's nice!" I called to my sister, who was searching for the room's light switch. "And I'm glad there's a rug so we can have another layer under our mats."

"Though that's not much added padding," she pointed out, looking down at the old, thinning Persian rug.

After a few moments, we heard the elevator doors open. Friends and acquaintances following my project started to arrive, several driving more than an hour to attend.

I introduced myself to our facilitator, Eric J. Christopher, MSMFT, CHT, a Marriage & Family Therapist as well as a Certified Hypnotherapist, as soon as he arrived. He had driven down for the workshop having only spoken with me via email. Tall, thin and blond with a voice like Casey Kasem, Eric invited us to pull our wicker chairs and sofas into a tighter circle.

"Hello," he greeted the group once we had all arrived. "I'm so happy to be here today. I want to start by telling you a little about me," he stated, gesturing at his chest and pacing. "In my practice, I do about two-thirds of my work in past life regressions and life between lives. The other third, I spend on present life healing. My belief is that pain in this life has its roots in the past. People come to me and I tell them 'we can heal that.' I am a true believer in emotional healing. And how did I get to that point? Well, my father was a Methodist pastor. We certainly didn't talk about reincarnation. Yet, when I graduated from college in 1988, I found myself in Taiwan teaching English. From there, I traveled to Nepal and India. In Calcutta,

I worked at the Mother Teresa House for the Destitute and Dying at the age of twenty-four. I was told to go sit with a man because he was about to die. I didn't know what I could offer, other than company, but I sat with him. He was speaking in Bengali; I did not understand anything. But that didn't matter. He reached out his arms to me... and he died in my arms."

Kolkata, formerly Calcutta, is located just 400 miles from that Crown Chakra point at Mount Kalish, by the way. It is also where Mother Teresa's tomb was located.

I felt the group sinking deeper into to the story. I glanced to Craig to see him shifting in his chair. I wondered if he was thinking about the car purchase he was planning to make directly after the workshop and regression. I turned back to Eric.

"When he died, the heat—the light—left," Eric explained. "I found myself wondering, 'what just left?' I knew that energy could never be destroyed, so I guessed it to be energy. But then where did it go if it could not be destroyed? Or had it been converted? Then, six years later, I read the book *Journey of Souls* by Dr. Michael Newton. That book changed my life," he declared.

For the next hour, in essence, we were attending an introductory class. Eric talked over experiences within his practice, patients he had helped in healing, books to learn more about the topic of reincarnation and finding past lives... Through it all, his passion was palpable. He lit up the room—literally jumping out of his seat several times at his own stories. He passed out handouts of individuals who believed they had found proof of the people they once were—records and gravestones and family members.

"The evidence is all there," Eric told us. "In fact, there is a lawyer from Australia named Victor Zammit. He wrote an entire book citing evidence that could be used in a court of law to determine if the afterlife existed or not. His case was and continues to be irrefutable, as far as I know. His book is called, *A Lawyer Presents the Evidence of the Afterlife*. He also has a weekly "Afterlife Report" that you can subscribe to receive each Friday. It is really great stuff."

I scribbled a note. Next up on my reading list. Sounded like my kind of angle.

"Personally, one of my favorite sessions was when a young man and woman came to visit me for hypnotherapy regarding a phobia. The young man handed me a note on a piece of paper. It said, 'She can't even hear the words out loud without having a reaction, but she is here to work on her fear of needles.'"

I glanced over to share a look with Craig, who was seated three people down from me. I, too, had a needle phobia. One that had caused me to seek out a birth center rather than a hospital in which to have our children, just to avoid all the needles.

Eric pushed his blond hair back, standing for a moment in front of the oscillating fan. "Within the session, the young woman saw herself in a past life that took place in an old-fashioned mental institution. One in which they performed electroshock therapy without any anesthesia. One in which she was tormented with needles full of various drugs and therapies. It was terrible for her to witness and relive in her mind, but when she came out of the hypnosis, she seemed lighter, more at ease. I didn't hear anything for months, but then, I received a message from them. It was from the young man. He wrote me to say that her phobia had all but been cured. She no longer feared needles as she once had."

I thought about my own needle phobia. I hadn't seen a single needle in any of my past life visions.

Eric continued, "And it had given her so much relief, that now the young man wished to visit me for his own mental setback. He told me that he suffered from a terrible fear of people leaving him, of being abandoned, left alone. That it affected his relationships and quality of life. That he wanted to know why he was so afraid of abandonment when, in this life, he had not truly experienced it. He also wanted to know why he chain-smoked so much."

I let my eyes wander over the group. I was curious what everyone thought so far. Hopeful they weren't feeling like Eric's passion was bordering on preachy. Though every face mirrored the glow sans workout, thanks to the lack of airflow in the old building, everyone appeared to be listening.

Eric crouched to sit in the chair at the head of the room, still telling the tale, but just before he reached the pink cushion on the wicker, he jumped back up to standing. "And when I put this young man under hypnosis, when I administered his past life regression, his story was unforgettable. He saw himself as a man; a husband and father. His wife was distant, uninvolved, void of emotion or character. He saw himself caring for their two children. Then when I asked him to view where he lived, he stopped. He told me he was in front of the house and the door was open but he did not want to go in."

My mind filled in the blanks. I already knew how it ended. I wasn't sure if I knew because of the empath in me or some touch of claircognizance or just watching too many movies, but I accurately guessed the ending.

Eric's hands were in the air in front of his body, waving as he spoke. "He went in anyway. He went in and walked up the stairs. He didn't want to, but he did. He opened the first door and saw his son... dead. Opened the next door, saw his daughter, also dead. Knew that his wife had done it. She was dead, too. His entire family was gone. When I asked him to view how that life ended, it was a sad scene. He was sitting on the curb, smoking cigarette after cigarette, in shock and mourning. He eventually drank and smoked himself to death, never filling the void of abandonment within himself. So I asked him to go—in the spirit world—go and call upon the souls of those who had been his children. To reunite. To have them release him from the guilt and pain he felt... And he did." Eric dropped his hands down for the first time in the story, visibly relieved. "And I got another message from him, months down the line. He had been able to move forward in his commitments to others. He had been able to lessen his smoking. He felt better and his fear was gone."

Eric picked up a printed piece of paper and read us the young man's actual message. It was moving.

After a few more stories from Eric's experiences, as well as other book recommendations, it was time for a bathroom break and preparation for the past life regression. The time had come.

On the long, dim walk to the nearest restroom, I quizzed my friends. How was it so far? Were they upset they had come? Had he made anyone uncomfortable? Did it seem too preachy? I had a fear of being seen as the "newly-saved" who was dragging people unwilling to church.

A coworker of mine summed best, "I like that he said we could take what we wanted and leave the rest. I am secure in my beliefs so I'm not about to throw it all away, but I'm finding portions of what he's saying interesting and plausible and I'm taking some things from it."

The majority agreed as we made our way back to the room.

Craig had already started pushing back the furniture for everyone when I walked back into the lounge. I sent him good vibes, seeing he was unrolling his mat way in the back, outside of the large area rug.

Becky rolled out her mat near my feet, with my coworker on one side and friend-since-seventh-grade on the other. While we all situated our mats, pillows and blankets, I stared up at the uncovered windows. Preferring the darkness of night like all of my previous regressions, I folded a corner of my blanket over my eyes.

Eric had a different approach than Aileen. Where Aileen's regression usually lasted just over an hour, Eric's would be less than forty-five minutes. Where Aileen guided by beginning in present-life memories, working back through the womb and into 'before the womb,' Eric preferred visualizing a tunnel past a garden. Both used singing bowls and both had melodic, chanting voices that allowed for deep meditation.

As Eric was asking the group to imagine sending the conscious mind up into a balloon, as it would no longer be needed, mine wasn't ready. My conscious mind was chattering at an intense speed.

Should I have invited so many people? Did everyone think this was crazy? Was the cement floor going to cause Craig's back to spaz out? Would my sister see anything? Did my feet stink over by Becky?

So many thoughts.

And then in the midst of the chattering... I was just 'there.'

I had heard that the more meditation was practiced the easier it was to achieve. I suppose that was true for me because mid-sentence, my conscious mind was just muted. I was in a scene. A familiar scene.

I dropped in, sinking in wild emotions. I was standing next to a turbulent ocean, having just gotten off my gray horse with white speckles on her flanks. I was filled with dread and fear, already sure something terrible had happened. I looked down the dock to a fishing boat that I knew was my father's.

I had thin, wispy red hair that the wind forced over my young face like a web. I had freckles. I was wearing a thick, cable-knit, cream-colored sweater. I knew it was my older brother's. It had a hole in the left side near the armpit where he'd gotten it caught on a fence.

I was sobbing so hard my hair was sticking to my tears and dripping nose.

But then Eric asked to see where we lived. It was hard to pull the fifteen-year-old girl from the scene, away from the raging waves and emotions. It was like she wanted to hang in that moment, torturing herself... like she thought she deserved the pain.

Reluctantly, I (as the girl) looked at my home. There was a large yard filled with prairie grass and small wildflowers. A few sheep grazed around. There were children playing and screaming in the yard. It was a rectangle-shaped, brown house with white around the windows and doors. It had the cedar-shingle look, like in Cape Cod, but the shingles were a deep brown rather than gray. At the top, there was a row of dormer windows sticking out the roof; the one on the right, for my bedroom.

When I was asked to envision a meal, I saw a table with eight chairs in front of a large fireplace. My dear papa sat at the head of the table, right in front of the fireplace. Behind him was a swinging door into the kitchen. We sat in order of age, with my older brother at the corner nearest my papa. I thought his name was Johan. Next was me. Beside me, my sister Birgitte. I wondered what my name was. It wasn't clear. Gillian came to mind. I saw my mother going in and out of the swinging door beside the fireplace, making sure everyone had what they needed. I was eating potatoes with peas, I think. And meat that I didn't like. Mutton came to mind, but I didn't know what mutton was in my conscious mind. (I found later that it was sheep, which was fitting since the family owned sheep.) There were nine of us, but only eight places at the table. I knew my mother waited until someone finished before she had a place to sit. I didn't feel bad about that. I didn't feel close to my mother or seem to feel sympathy for her. I was filled with teenage hormones and anger, because no one ever noticed me except my papa. The name Papa Jorgen came to mind. I wondered if we were the Jorgensons or if his name was Jorgen. I couldn't place our location or the time.

I looked at my beloved father when Eric asked us to view who we were closest to in the lifetime. I saw Papa's once-black hair and beard, peppered with white and gray. He was a large man with a barrel chest. He had shining, kind blue eyes with laugh lines at the corners. His face was leathery from being out at sea, in the fishing boat. When he laughed, he tipped his head back and laughed with his entire body, shoulders and belly heaving. I loved his laugh. I loved him. I was enamored with him. I wanted to be with him every moment, but knew he was gone for long periods of time. When he was home, he'd sit in front of the fireplace with a pipe and tell us stories about mermaids and shipwrecks and amazing things he'd see out in the wild waters. I loved his stories! Sopped them up. Obsessed about them. Wrote some of them down in my diary.

When asked to see how we spent a lot of time in the life, I saw Gillian leaning under a thick tree at the back of the yard, watching all the little ones; her siblings (after switching to a third-person watching point of view). I knew she didn't care about any of them. She resented them. They were the reason she was often ignored. There were so many of them and always needing something. She looked up from her book to see a younger brother—around age three or four—picking at a sheep.

I became her again and saw the view from her eyes. I was too lazy and annoyed to get up so I grabbed a rock that filled my entire palm and chucked it at him. I felt the heft of the rock and the jolt of my tiny arm. The rock hit him in the back of the shoulder. I was proud I hit him. I didn't even notice if he cried or not. I couldn't be bothered to care. I hated everyone—or at least was bitter and mean toward everyone.

My conscious mind couldn't believe what a horrible, teenage brat she was.

Then, when the group was prompted to view a bad part in the life, I already knew it was my father's death. I was right back there at the first moment; at the docks, panting in that thick sweater with the ocean filling my head along, with the pounding of fear in my ears. I somehow knew that I'd had a dream that Papa was going to die. I had a flashback of myself in a white, ankle-length nightgown, sweaty and terrified after a dream. A dream that had told the future. A dream in which my papa had died while fishing.

I'd told my mother; begged and pleaded that she not let him go. I told her I *knew* he would not come back, but she didn't listen to me or take my words seriously. She never even told Papa about my dream. But I had known.

Standing at the dock, I watched him laughing with his

mates in his blue sweater that made his eyes look like jewels from a treasure chest under the sea. He didn't notice me watching him, but that was the last time I ever saw him.

I rode my horse to the dock day after day, waiting for him to return, already knowing he was never coming back.

And then the day the ship docked, I saw his mates with bowed heads and removed hats...

I screamed! I sobbed! I felt the worst mourning pain I had ever known in any life! I hopped on my horse. I was hysterical. I couldn't see with the tears and wind whipping my red hair over my eyes. I knew my horse knew the way home. I jumped off the bare back before the horse was slowed enough. I burst through the door and ran right up to my mother in the parlor and accused her and blamed her and hated on her. (It was so terrible for me, as Gina, to watch.) I wanted to make her feel worse than I did, which was the baddest of bads.

She remained calm, as usual. She was blank. She went into the kitchen and I heard her sob. Instead of going in to comfort her, my mind shouted, "Good! That's what you deserve for letting him die!"

The sound of her sobbing in the other room made my current-self cry from my motionless position on the floor of the spirituality center. It was terrible.

When we were asked to move forward, I saw our large family leaving the house by the seaside and moving into a crowded city. In a very narrow, cramped, blackish building. It was the hot, small apartment of my mother's sister. We slept four to a bed. I don't think my older brother was there. Birgitte may have already been married, though she would have only been around sixteen, because she wasn't there either.

I wrote stories and read books and blamed myself for not trusting my premonition. I was hollow and hated living. One day, I was reading a book—about ghosts, I think—and I was hit by a car while crossing the confined street with my face hidden by a hardcover.

It was an old-style car with large, round headlamps. People around me screamed. There didn't seem to be a roof on the vehicle because I could hear the driver chanting, "Oh no! Oh no! Oh no!" over and over. A crowd gathered. I was already hovering above the frail seventeen-year-old body. My thoughts were, "Good. One less mouth for my mother to feed. One less child in the apartment. It will be better for everyone now that I'm gone."

Then, when we went to the spirit world, things were different. I was her *and* I was me. We were two, something I had never experienced. Gina was scolding her a bit. Telling her how wrong many of our thoughts and actions had been. But she was so emotionally hurt and I knew that in being ignored, she had heightened her insecurities and worries to outrageous, frantic, unrealistic, crazed levels. So much estrogen and emotion! I took her young hand in mine. I saw it and felt it. It was small in mine. I petted it and reassured her... "It's okay now. We're so much better now. We have come so far. We're not like that anymore. We know much more and everything is really okay."

I felt both of us fill with relief and the hand in mine vaporized away.

Then I was hovering upward. I came up to the spirit guide I had envisioned in every other experience; came up to him as if I were on an elevator. As I was approaching, I saw a sad shake of his head. "We're done here, kid," he said. Then he used his thumb to motion upward and I kept going up. I shouted down, "I just lost my father. I don't want to lose you, too!" He was half-smiling and just shrugged.

When I got up to the next level, I joined the sea of yellow

light. It was like all of the other times I'd seen the spirit world, but as if I were seeing more of it. As if there was an entire ocean of yellowish energy flowing in the sky. One orb of light dripped down and was absorbed into the whole; went back into the oneness, no longer separate. It traveled along with the flow. Orbs dripped out, others dripped back in. I sensed it was a resting place.

I asked Gillian on my own: Was there a reason I was seeing the life story now?

She looked at me with a face full of bitter teen angst and rolled her eyes. "Trust yourself?" she asked more than said, too annoyed by me to give a real answer.

There was little time to process before getting the room ready for the next rental, who inexplicably had a dog with them who kept sniffing in the doorway. Our time was up. I did ask the group how many had seen something useful. All but three raised a hand; both Craig and my sister being among those who had experienced *nothing*. Disappointment and guilt crept in. I felt bad for asking them to lie on the floor for an hour without experiencing anything mesmerizing.

After sharing a few stories—my young coworker who saw a life as a Vietnam vet, a woman who saw a medicine woman living in a cave, two sisters who had both seen farmers—the group dispersed. After hugging and thanking everyone, I was pleased to hear most say they would try it again. I was relieved it hadn't been too much.

It was swelteringly hot outside and my dark cloth interior made my sister and I sweat all the way to pick up the kids.

Once we picked them up and arrived home, Becky asked if she could stop by. I was happy to say yes, as she lived mere blocks away from us, but didn't get together as often as we would have liked.

The three of us recapped the day and our experiences and thoughts on the whole thing. Craig called from the dealership. He was purchasing a car and would be gone most of the day.

Feeling mostly sure I had made up the Gillian life in some sort of lucid dream, I began searching for the names that had appeared. Not consciously aware of the origins of any of the names, I was startled as they compiled:

> GILLIAN: *Danish, Norwegian, Swedish*
> JØRGEN: *Danish, Norwegian, Faroese*
> BIRGITTE: *Danish, Norwegian*
> JOHAN: *Norwegian, Danish, Dutch, Swedish*

Denmark had a "correct" feel to it. I searched "Denmark house by the ocean" and not too far in, found an image of a brown house with white trim and dormer windows near the ocean.

But, at least for me, the experience had not seemed real enough. The name of the car dealership Craig had been going to? Gilly's. The name of the newly voted-in president at work, as well as someone I interviewed for this book? Birgitte. The beloved Papa who seemed as if he could have been Becky's father? Black hair and a similar smile. And the day before the past life regression, I had written the section about meeting with Melissa Divine, and her implication that I might harbor some sort of gift. Never before had a past life been so convenient.

I talked it all through with Becky. "I have no doubt in my mind that it is real," she stated.

"How can you be so sure?" I whined. "I want to be that sure... it's exhausting, constantly arguing both sides and deciphering and skeptically searching for holes."

"That *does* sound exhausting. Just stop doing that."

My sister and I laughed, her chiming in, "That's just not us."

Becky said, "That part when Eric was talking about seeing signs from loved ones who have passed away made me think of my grandma. I always know when I see a red cardinal, it's her saying hi."

"Really?" I interjected, thinking back to my reassuring bird sighting. "Well, maybe she flew down the block to say hi, because I felt like a cardinal was stalking me a while back and I wasn't sure why."

Becky was smiling. "That was Grandma!"

I shook my head, always captivated by her certainty. "So you didn't see *anything*?" I asked my sister at the other end of the table.

"Not really. I sensed black hair, felt it was hot. Looked down to see dry, cracked, dirt under me. But mostly, I kept thinking, 'There's nothing to see. I don't have anything to view.'"

"Strange. Well, I have heard that sometimes souls have to rest. They just... hang out in the energy field and recoup before going again."

She shrugged. "Maybe."

I looked to Becky. "I guess that makes us the schmucks with our hands in the air, 'We'll go again! Pick us! We'll go!'"

Becky laughed. "Sounds like us."

"Yes, but how do we get off this crazy thing?" I asked. "What if the Buddhists are still celebrating Buddha's Parinirvāna because he is the one and only soul who has ever completed this gargantuan puzzle?"

"Yikes..." my sister mumbled.

I bit my lip and shook my head.

"Craig didn't see anything either?" Becky asked.

"Nothing."

"Well, when I forced my husband and daughter to go with me last year, neither of them saw anything either. But they are left-brain people. Afterwards, we talked about reading. Like, when you read, do you see the whole world like you're in it?"

"Yes, definitely," I replied.

"I don't," my sister added. "It's just words that sort of make sense. I don't see it all like a movie."

"Huh..." I uttered. "Well, Craig doesn't like reading for the same reason. You think there's a connection?"

"Maybe," Becky concluded. "You and I are very right-brained."

"That we are. And yours was good?" I asked, watching the light shine on Becky's pretty brown hair.

"Oh, yes!"

"When we were coming out of it, I sat up and saw a grin on your face. I could tell it was a good one."

"Well, like Eric suggested, I went in with an intention. I asked why I struggle so much with food... and I ended up seeing a terribly detailed life in which I died from starvation and thirst on a deserted island. My spirit guide assured me I would never again be that hungry, that I would never starve. I feel great!" she declared.

"Huh..." I said, thinking back to Memphis. "You know, when you say it that way... and the way Eric was talking about healing phobias, maybe I was thinking about the elevator thing all wrong."

"What elevator thing?" my sister asked.

"Well, throughout my life, I've gotten nervous on elevators.

After I saw the past life with Vinny who died by falling backwards down an elevator shaft, I expected to find the tallest free-standing elevator in Memphis a problem. But when I went up... nothing. I thought it was because it was all glass—I could see the beams and out through the building. But if this whole 'healing' thing is real... maybe I'm just no longer afraid of elevators?"

"Well, were you nervous in the elevator at the center? That was a creaky, old elevator!" Becky pointed out.

I thought a moment. "I mean... I wasn't. But it was only going down one floor."

"I think it worked," Becky said.

"I think it could just be a coincidence," my sister said.

"I think it's fun to think about," I finished.

Two days after the group regression, life was somewhat back to normal. We had a new vehicle, our daughter knew about the new school and I had "graduated" from my twelve-week nutrition program with twenty-one pounds lost. I knew my search was coming to a close. I had researched and interviewed for nearly nine months. When what I thought was to be my final interview fell through, I was "focusing on the 3D" for a bit, not overly concerned with who my last voice would be. But that's when I saw a Facebook post that made me cry out "What!" in disbelief. It was a post from my longtime friend from elementary school, Britt. And her amazing story had just become that much more unbelievable.

Though we had tried to connect in January, April and May, Britt and I had not found a time to speak. Her life had recently become all the more complicated with her middle-aged brother's sudden cancer diagnosis.

Britt and I hadn't spoken in years, though we were connected through social media like many totally-best-friends-in-the-nineties tended to be. Her younger sister had lost a valiant fight against her own liver, in addition to Britt's car accident, so to hear about the family facing more tragic health news made the breath catch in my throat.

I texted Britt's cell phone, seeing if she would be free to speak in about an hour. I was delighted when she agreed!

Before the interview, I couldn't help but look through her younger sister's Facebook page. Though she had been gone since 2010, her wall was anything but vacant. Visitors left messages... often. "Popping by to say hello," "Can't wait to be with you in the future," "Thanks for visiting my dreams," were a few of the themes within the messages. There were so many messages about dreams throughout the years. It made sadness well up inside of me. Every year, there was a string of "Happy birthday" posts. And there, back in 2013, was a post by Britt to her sister, "Broken pelvis (in three places) and a broken sacrum. I'm trying to be super strong and work hard so I can be home for Christmas." Tears filled my eyes. Here was the reason Britt had made my interview list—her car accident.

I called her up and, though it had been years since we'd heard each other speak, her voice made me smile. "Hello, long-lost friend!" I called into my cell phone.

"Well, hi there!" she replied, her voice filled with shiny optimism, like always, it seemed.

"I just saw your post about your brother being pronounced cancer-free! I am so thrilled and shocked!" So far everything out of my mouth had been said at exclamation point level. I evened out and we began our interview in the sliver of time between a work deadline and picking up my son from preschool.

I'm alive because of prayer

The Christian

B RITT BRILL IS a high school special education teacher, working with students on the autism spectrum.

"Tell me a little about the past decade or so," I requested. "How would you describe your background?"

"Well, I'm a special education teacher, but I started out to be a math teacher," she said of herself. "When I was a freshman, my mom told me about a job with an 'autistic child.' Yes, that's what she said, though that's no longer politically correct, but I know it was those words because I remember replying that I didn't even know what the word 'autistic' meant back in 2000. 'You'll be great at it!' she said. It was working with a boy on the spectrum who had never had a therapist before. He had behaviors that made caring for him difficult. But as the summer progressed, we really connected. When I told him I was leaving to go back to school, he took my hand and kissed it saying, 'Goodbye, my princess. I'll miss you.'"

"Aww," I cooed.

She let out a small laugh. "Yeah. I changed my major. I ended up getting my Masters in special education."

"Wow."

"It was actually when I was driving from school to my job as an autism specialist when I crashed…" She trailed off.

"Oh... well... before we talk about that, do you believe that humans have a soul?" I asked.

"Yes...?"

I chuckled. "Was that a yes with a question mark or a yes with a period?"

"A yes with an exclamation point!" she restated with a small laugh. "That's how God made us."

"And what do you believe happens to the soul when we die?"

"I believe we go to Heaven and are reunited with loved ones and dance in streets of gold!" she exaggerated in a fun tone. "Okay, I don't know all the things, but I think it's perfect with no evil. Just goodness. That's what I've known since I was a girl."

"Did you grow up with these beliefs?" I asked, knowing the answer.

"I was baptized Lutheran, but yes, I've always been Christian."

"And... now to the accident," I prompted. "Can you tell me about your near-death experience and how it impacted you physically and spiritually?"

She took a breath and began her story. I got the feeling she had been asked to talk about her account on many occasions. "On December 10, 2013... wait, let me back up," she said, restarting the order of events. "I was due to have my first child in July. I had him and two weeks later, my husband got a text message saying he was fired."

"By text?" I repeated in disbelief.

"Yes. So we were down to one income. And when he told me, I was excited. Actually excited. Why? Because I knew my baby would have the best parent possible staying home with him. I know this isn't a normal reaction, but every situation has a positive and a negative. It was the positive. So, just four weeks after our son was born, I went back to work. I worked two jobs and he became a stay-at-home-dad. I worked at my autism job on nights and weekends. On that December night in 2013, I was between jobs. I was done teaching and had stayed for a meeting. I decided to take a back road because it was shorter, quicker. Bray Road in Elkhorn." She paused. It seemed like she was waiting for a response. "You don't know Bray Road?" she asked after a moment.

"No... should I?" I asked.

"There's a movie about it. The Beast of Bray Road in Elkhorn, Wisconsin," she explained.

"I don't know it," I told her, too engrossed in the story to stop for a search. "I'll look it up," I assured her, underlining the term.

Britt continued. "So I was between jobs and it had snowed, but the roads were dry. I came around a corner and there was a snow drift." Her words picked up pace. She started talking so quickly my hands could barely keep up on my notepad. "The snow drift caused my car to fly off the road. I was headed toward an enormous tree. And I knew I was going to die," she said with full certainty. "I just knew it. This was how it was going to end. I started praying for my husband to find a new wife, a wife who would love him and love my children. Praying my children would be loved once I was gone..."

I gulped down my panic, so loud I heard it through the cell phone speaker.

Britt continued in her hurried pace, "Then I stopped and thought, '*What in the world am I praying for*?' I switched gears and shouted three times, 'Lord, protect me! Lord, protect me! Lord, protect me!' And... I wasn't even knocked unconscious. Oh, I hit that tree. My car was smashed. But at that point,

I didn't feel any pain. I remember looking up and seeing a car coming. I thought, 'Thank God! Someone is coming.' But then I started worrying she would hit the snowbank and also hit my car. But then she drove past... she was on her cell phone... she waved to me," she trailed off in disbelief.

"What!" I yelped.

"Sorry, I'm going to cry," Britt continued. "So when I saw another car coming, I couldn't believe it. It was a back road and another car was coming past me," her voice was trembling. "In the next car, was one of the miracles. It was a coworker." She breathed loudly. "I didn't know why he was there or where my cell phone was. I knew things were bad and I asked to use his. I called my husband, but he didn't answer, so I called my dad. My dad answered and I said, 'Dad, I was just in an accident!' and he said, 'I know!'"

"Wha... How?" I blurted. "How could he have known?"

"Just another of the strange things surrounding my accident," Britt stated. "My husband had been calling me just as I hit the snowbank. Somehow—somehow—the impact answered my phone. My poor husband heard it all... He heard me scream, heard the car crashing into the tree... he heard everything," she finished in an earnest tone.

"I cannot imagine! How is that even possible?" I cried, sad that I had never known her full story before. "I can't imagine how terrifying that would have been!"

"And he didn't know where I was," she whispered. "He heard it all happen, but he didn't know where I was. He was calling the police and the hospital and preparing everything while I was on the phone with my dad," she continued. "My coworker stayed with me until the ambulance came. The paramedics looked at me and my little car and said, 'You should not be alive.' And I knew that was true. They had to cut the car to get me out onto a stretcher... and that's when I felt the pain."

I shuddered. So engrossed in the story, I was burning in a hot bed of empathy.

"After the long and painful ride to the hospital, I arrived and my parents were already there. My husband was there. They... it's like they knew I was in an accident before *I knew*," she described. "After some testing, I saw the look on the doctor's face. I had just one question on my mind and I asked him, 'When will I walk again?' He looked down at me and said, 'I'm afraid it's more like *if* you walk again.'"

"No!" I called out, trying to recall whether all the Facebook pictures I'd seen through the years had ever depicted her standing or walking.

"I had a newborn baby at home. I had a husband with no job. And now I would have no job. My next thought was to my husband. I said to him, 'You did not sign up for this. You can go if you need to.' But he looked at me like I was crazy. Of course, he stayed with me. He thought I was ridiculous for saying it."

I was nodding while writing, my hand cramping at the vehemence of the story.

"So the doctor came back with the results. My pelvis was broken in three places, my coccyx was broken, my sacrum was broken and I had a lacerated liver."

"But your legs were okay?" I asked.

"They were. Bruised, but okay. But because my younger sister had died from liver problems, when my mother heard that word... something happened to her. It wasn't good."

Again, I shook my head in pity, knowing how kindhearted and loving Britt's mother was, feeling for her as a fellow mom.

"So then the doctor told me I was facing four months in

the hospital. It was December, I had an infant at home... I was going to miss his first Christmas," she stated, the tears coming back.

"No!" the Mama Bear in me cried out.

"I was transferred to a hospital in Janesville, Wisconsin. I got there and the next day they said, 'Let's get you up and walking!' I liked their enthusiasm and optimism, but it was terrifying. I told them what the other hospital had said, but they told me they just needed to see." She took a breath. A first pause in a long while. "So they sat me up... and I fainted. I passed out from the pain. It was so intense I can't even describe it. So then I was on more pain meds... with a newborn at home. A newborn who was refusing formula. He just wouldn't take formula," she reiterated. "And that's when another of my miracles happened. Milk just started showing up! From as far away as Kentucky, mothers were sending me their milk to feed my baby."

I felt the tears well up again. It was such a beautiful display of humanity. Of sisterhood.

Britt continued her story, "So you know how easy it is to walk?" she asked rhetorically. "Well, I kept working and trying... and I couldn't even lift my toe. I was telling it to move and it wouldn't. I was there for about a week before I was transferred back to Elkhorn. It was hard for my family to visit so far, with the snow storms and all. I was no longer in trauma so they let me go back. When I got there, they told me again, 'You will be here for three to four months.' But you know what? I got out on December twenty-first."

"No! How? How did you? Britt, you are amazing!"

"I had lots of people praying for me and backing me up and asking for me to be home for Christmas. I had a walker. A walker I named Texas Ranger... Walker, Texas Ranger, because everyone needs a little Chuck Norris in their life." She let out a laugh.

I also laughed, enjoying the image of Chuck Norris holding her up for Christmas. Loving her instinct to make the best even of the worst.

"But I knew even if I got home, I wouldn't be able to get into the house. At the hospital and in therapy, we practiced stairs. They were small and I couldn't do them. The ones at my house were steep; it was an old house. And so came another miracle. While I was at the hospital, volunteers from our church came out and rebuilt our stairs."

"Oh, wow!" I chimed in again.

"We had no jobs and many medical bills, but I went home. And four months after the accident, I was not still in the hospital. I was walking again," she stated with pride. "But it was tough. To have a baby cry for you and not be able to run over and pick him up... But I was blessed. Because my husband was home. He helped me do therapy and helped with everything. But having a baby is motivation to work hard and get back to normal."

My head was shaking and I couldn't make it stop. "And did it all have a lasting effect on you—spiritually?"

"I've always been a Christian and I believed in the power of God, but I was hesitant to share it before. My accident has been a platform to talk about faith and to offer to others in a time of need or to celebrate the miracles."

"You have such a positive outlook."

"I don't know how else to be," she stated with ease. "Without my faith, I wouldn't be alive. Without prayer, I wouldn't be alive. Or maybe I would be alive, but not walking. I asked. I prayed. So many of us did. I gave testimony in our church. I was invited to my husband's family church in Stevens Point,

Wisconsin because they had all been praying for me and following my story from afar. Months after the accident, they invited me to speak and I walked up to the front! I walked up and gave my testimony of prayer. Everyone was so excited. I was there. I was able to be a mom to my kids."

"So powerful... Did you ever have any sort of near-death vision or experience?" I was curious to know.

"Getting in that accident and shouting..." she trailed off. "I don't know why I shouted that three times. But I *knew*, I was being protected. They say your life flashes before your eyes—that is true. It couldn't have been more than three seconds, but it felt so long. It felt like so much. I thought about my kids living without me. It was the fastest and the slowest moment before my tiny car hit that big tree. It was so smashed. You know, I go back and I see my tree—I call it *my* tree," she chuckled at herself. "I go back on the anniversary of the accident and take a picture. To conquer the fear. To remember the protecting. I'm sure you've seen the pictures I've posted. You can look... it is just a *massive* tree," she told me.

I looked up the photo she'd referenced. There she was, standing next to the very tree that had almost claimed her life. In typical cheerful Britt fashion, she was wearing a bright yellow peacoat. It contrasted the horrific, ripped bark and what looked like claw marks across the trunk of the tree. She was so brave. The bravest.

"So after facing it head on, are you afraid of death?" I asked.

"I wouldn't say I'm afraid," she answered. "It's not the end and I know I'll go to Heaven and that this is just a small part. I know it's going to happen; I just hope I don't have to face it again soon."

"Me neither! How old were you when you were in the accident?"

"Just thirty-one."

My head went back into a sympathetic shake. "Okay, so what do you think about reincarnation? Do you think we come back to live again?"

"I think we go to Heaven. No, I don't think we come back here."

"Thoughts on signs? Do you believe there are forces leaving signs to be seen?"

"Through prayer, yeah. When I am being led through prayer, I think there's a best possible way through and that there will be signs."

I jotted down her answered. "Now, if we can just talk about your brother... wow!"

She let out a small laugh. "We asked for him to be healed, and he was," she stated. "Another miracle. It started on October 16, 2018 at 3:45pm, when I heard the words I didn't want to hear, yet they could never be unheard. Tumor. My brother had a tumor. The words that took me to my knees. It stung, like the cold Wisconsin wind. I couldn't breathe. They would be doing more testing to determine if it was cancerous. Ten days later, he got the call. Cancer. Acute myeloid leukemia was the diagnosis. In November, we all packed up and headed on a family vacation to his favorite spot to visit with his two children. We spent a week together as a family, enjoying time with one another, away from the hustle and bustle of life... We laughed, took pictures, soaked it all in! After that, he was checked in to the hospital to start his chemo treatments. Lots of visits to the hospital followed. Thanksgiving in the hospital, Christmas in the hospital, New Year's Eve in the hospital..."

"I'm just so sorry," I couldn't help but interject.

"On January 1, 2019, we stayed in Madison to be near his hospital. When I walked in, my brother's wife pulled me aside.

She said the doctors had given up hope. There was nothing more they were going to do. I fell down crying. But I didn't give up hope! I asked my brother if I could pray with him. He was Christian as well, but we had never prayed together. And never out loud. He said, 'Yeah, I don't have anything else.' So we did. I don't even know how long I prayed. I just prayed and prayed until I felt peace."

"You are so incredible," I told my friend in the neighboring state.

"Prayer is incredible. Asking and receiving miracles. Seeing my big brother that vulnerable... hearing him say, 'I don't want to die. I'm not ready to die.'" She fell silent a moment, composing herself. "Well, after we prayed, he told me, 'I'm not done. Let's find a new hospital.' This was after he had told everyone he was not going to seek out a second opinion. A few days later, Milwaukee responded that they would take him. They had a plan. He needed a bone marrow transplant. They found the type he needed for a perfect match, but only had one person in the database—who was completely unreachable; thought to have moved out of the country. We prayed. Most hospitals only allowed a bone marrow transplant from someone younger than sixty. My dad was sixty-eight. We were told that the hospital my brother had just transferred to was the only hospital to allow transplants from people up to age seventy! My dad was tested and he was a close match, the closest match available. My brother needed five million bone marrow stem cells. In the retrieval, they got more than six million from my dad. It was enough."

"I remember that post," I said, searching her wall. I found her call to action from February. She had written:

"This has been a long journey and I recognize that it

isn't over yet. Today is a day that I watch my hero give a gift that is truly unmatched—the gift of a second chance for my brother. Please take a moment to pray for my dad, to pray for my brother and his family, to pray for my mom, my sister, and me. To pray for our entire family. We know that prayer is powerful and that in Matthew 18:20 it says, "Where two or more are gathered, there I am with them." Please gather with us and pray for full restoration for my brother, for wisdom for all of the doctors involved, for peace to flood over my dad, as he undergoes his treatment today. Gather with us in prayer."

I had sent out a private, sincere ask that day. Along with so many others. We had collectively asked.

Britt continued, "Before the transplant, my brother's white blood cell count was zero. Literally none. His kids hadn't been allowed in the room to see him in like a month. We all had to wear masks. If we had any sense of a symptom, we could not visit because we could kill him. But within a week, his white blood cell count skyrocketed! Faster than anticipated. Two weeks later, he came home."

"After only two weeks?" It sounded farfetched. I couldn't believe the family's experiences.

"Six months ago, I walked into a hospital to hear the doctor say they were giving up on my brother, and that I should say my goodbyes to another sibling. I didn't believe it, so I asked the doctor myself, and he confirmed: They didn't have hope he would survive, just three months after being diagnosed. This past Wednesday, I cried as I enjoyed a day at an amusement park with my brother! And today, we received word that he is *free* of cancer! I praise God! He has done amazing things for me and my family and I want that for each and every person that I know," Britt told me. "I would have lost my brother and I would have lost my mom... she couldn't go through it all again."

"I am so relieved! What did you do to celebrate?"

"We did what we do—gathered together on Sunday. Just the way we always have and always will."

I didn't want the conversation to end, but I glanced at the clock to see I was already eight minutes late to pick up my son from preschool. I apologized and promised to do better at communication, then flew out the door—perhaps rightfully cautious driving across town to get him.

Soon after my interview with Britt, my social media scroll was halted yet again by a relevant message. It was after ten at night and I was waiting for Craig to finish brushing his teeth before bed. I was not in the mood for another piece of the puzzle, yet I found it regardless. It said, "'Do not be afraid' is mentioned in the Bible 365 times, one for every day of the year."

I don't know why I never got used to receiving, but it always caught me off guard. I'd rounded a full circle once again. From my first pertinent past life lesson from Jean the Canadian, years prior to the final chapter of my spiritual journey, the day before I finished this book. It made me feel gratitude. And I hoped that gratitude truly was a link to the spiritual world.

I had no idea how my subconscious had quoted the Bible when I had only ever read select passages from the Bible, never been a part of Bible study groups. I wondered why humans needed to be reassured once per day. Why were we so afraid?

But I took in the reassurance and the reminder.

Craig came out of the bathroom none-the-wiser. I hugged him for a long time. Like until he was uncomfortable. It was the best.

What I learned along the way

IN THE HEAT of July, under the roar of a box fan and a neighboring lawn mower, I completed my journey. Completed is the correct word; not ended. I typed up my last interview, closed my surveys, shelved my books. My semester of learning was coming to a close, but it wasn't ending. In fact, I had ten of the fifteen people from the group past life regression ask when the next one would be scheduled. I had Victor Zammit's book on its way from the great Amazon beyond. I had a string of people curious if they, too, could be interviewed and included in my humble compilation. I had the new avenue of right brain versus left brain to explore. And the synchronicities wouldn't stop.

While I was sitting on my couch watching the kids play, I felt like I was in a movie, the part when a dramatic, thundering zoom-in occurs. Hiding in plain sight among the Legos was a swirl. It was on the sail of a *Moana* Lego set, and it was THE swirl.

My fingers were swiping in the search bar so fast even autocorrect didn't know what I was asking. "Meaning of *Moana* swirl symbol" finally emerged.

Two words emerged: Koru and Taino. A Koru spiral is

meant to represent growth or new life. The Taino's swirl is a symbol of the Caribbean natives. Its meaning? Cosmic energy. Specifically, though, the clockwise swirl of the spiral used in *Moana* refers to the human experience through birth, life and resurrection.

Uncanny!

With information still coming to me, I thought about keeping it all open. But like so many intelligent people had said to me, that would be a bit too ambitious.

So, while I will continue to learn and ponder and experience, the journey has come to a natural conclusion. I found sprawling threads of connectivity. And I found a few answers. Of the dozen interviews I conducted, the themes were:

67% believed humans had a soul.
75% were not afraid of death.
41% believed in reincarnation.
67% believed in signs.

And that survey I created about souls? As of July 2019... not a great turnout. But I'm including a few points anyway, because I find the data thought-provoking, regardless of its usefulness.

From my survey, thirty-two people responded from ages ranging from under eighteen to over sixty-five, 79% being women, all but seven being from Minnesota (ah, smell the hotdish). To me, the most captivating portion of the survey was the answer to the question, "What do you believe happens to the soul after the body dies?" The winner, barely, was Christian Heaven, earning 31% of the vote, but reincarnation was selected by 28%. Only 4% believed that nothing happened after death, with the rest being unsure. Did my sample believe themselves to have lived before? A perfect tie. 44% said yes,

44% said no. The remaining selected other/don't know. One comment said, "I don't know that I've ever thought of this before," which I, of course, loved. I love thinking about new concepts and introducing new ideas to others.

Sixty-two percent said yes, they believe in guiding signs.

So where does that leave us?

After delving into the opinions and minds on several sides of the topic, I'm happy to say I came out the other side with at least one answer; a common thread woven throughout every opinion: Humans are here for the infatuating, infuriating, lovely experiences we share while we're alive.

Humans. That's it in a sum. We really do direct the fate of the world, we create the stories (supernatural and not), we speculate about what will happen after we die, we experience. Every day is and should be treated like the beautiful gift that it is. But that can't be the final point. Without each other to share experiences with, it seems we are less than we could be. Living life without shared experiences might be the spiritual equivalent to being an orb of energy floating around aimlessly, searching for our sea of light in which to reunite and never finding it.

So many of the past life stories I have been told included the theme of loneliness. Specifically, the idea that there were people all around but the loneliness still persisted. On more than one occasion, after sitting up from a group past life regression, I watched people cry while explaining the torture of this type of loneliness. I felt it myself in a majority of the lives I'd viewed. But it just doesn't have to be.

All we need to do is reach out and someone will be there. Just reach out a little bit and you will literally bump into someone else—whether it be online, at the store, at work, at home… (Okay, don't physically reach out and touch someone at a store. Not what I'm going for here.) But other humans are always there. If you ask. If you reach. It can't just be a hope. It needs to be an action.

I asked strangers to tell me about deep, personal beliefs and most of them did—happily! Seeming downright joyful that someone had seen them, asked them, included them, connected with them. And that is how I look at human interaction. We all have the possibility and opportunity to be a part of the same story, one colorful thread woven into the lap quilt of Mother Nature, Father Time and the swirling universe of possibility.

So have I changed? Has this search and conclusion changed me? Undoubtedly, yes. Though I have always been one to cherish moments, sometimes becoming weepy-sentimental about time passing, I try now to be brave. To accept. To ask for help. To receive. The lessons I have learned have changed how I parent, how I interact with loved ones, how I think about my time here on Earth, how I participate.

So we may be human-with-a-side-of-soul while we are here in the physical, but how about the non-physical? Non-physically, why can't we be orbs of energy, magnetized into one overarching, complete whole? A beautiful, creative, symphonic, positive whole. An ocean, or an infinite lake of light, that we all fit into, all belonging there. From the chaos and strife of life with illnesses and sacks of meat to lug around, with babies to nurture and teach (and drop off at school), with pain and suffering that we will all eventually flee. Because whether it is scientifically proven or general consensus or not... what is the harm in believing we go on to a shared place of peace and love, love and light? And who's to say it can't be here *and* there; inside and out?

For we have all been murderers, let us all forgive. And let us start by reaching out.

The seven changes

After completing my spiritual journey, I noted the changes that were made to my everyday life. Changes and beliefs that nudged me into a new version of myself. What did I learn?

DON'T BE AFRAID.

To write the book. To put yourself out there. To connect with a stranger. To believe. To trust yourself. The list goes on. Back in 2016 when I first received that message, it struck me like a slap across my face. Because I knew I lived in fear and I was being chastised. But, three years later, I'm proud to say I've been living up to it. I have been making fewer choices based on fear. And that's so freeing! Whether a message from the Bible or a message from my first past life vision of Jean the French-Canadian, I have consciously decided to live life with less fear. (There's still fear, don't get me wrong. Just less of it.)

CONNECT ONLINE.

If you want to learn, start with a search. Duh, right? But never underestimate the powerful connection that the good, the bad and the ugly of the world wide web provides. It connects thoughts, ideas, theories, people, beliefs—drop down a rabbit hole. Jump in. No matter how obscure a topic, the world will open and you will find like-minded others devoting their time to teaching and explaining. Words, videos, music, it's all there. Such as? There are 69 million videos on YouTube about past lives. You want it? You got it. (Humans are awesome.)

IT'S OKAY TO BE AN EMPATH.

Do you feel what others feel? Do you have to distance yourself from the dark and grim to protect yourself from harm? Accept that. Understand it. I no longer view it as an affliction. I view it as a gift. We have the ability to care from a personal place—from within. I have no trouble slipping into someone else's perspective. Does that make empaths more argumentative because it's so easy to see all sides? My friends would say yes. But does it also make us quick to stand up for injustice and unfounded judgment? You tell me.

NOT EVERYONE HAS THE FREEDOM TO BE OPEN-MINDED.

Walking the streets of Memphis, surrounded by so many churches, and hospitals founded by churches, and housing developments organized and cared for by churches... I did not feel a strong sense of choice. I realize it's a freedom to be able to talk and study and write about spiritual theory without fear of scary consequences. To *not* be burnt alive in a public square. We should not take that lightly. Nor should we judge those who haven't been afforded that kind of freedom.

SAVOR EXPERIENCES.

I know it's the cover story of every bro-gazine (I just coined that. Magazines for Bros.), but we do need to *live for today*! I think about the advice I was given—to savor running a bluff, snuggling a baby, the thrill of joys and tears and fears. Without experiences, what are we left with? Even if you believe we will turn to dust and there will be no afterlife, isn't that all the more reason to strive to experience all you can? (Hey, look at that. Yet another factor that makes us more alike than different.)

JUST ASK.

I cannot emphasize enough. Ask people, and people will answer. Ask the universe and somehow opportunities appear. Ask the higher spirit and sometimes even prayers about cancer are answered. I have incorporated this into my everyday life. I do not see the harm in asking anymore. I'd like to think I've achieved official AskHole status.

LIVE LIFE AS IF TODAY IS YOUR REVIEW.

I don't think it even matters whether it is real or not—living today like you will be sitting in a spiritual room in the sky rewatching every decision and word that hurt others is powerful. It also winds back around to karma. Perhaps it's time to send better things out there. Unfortunately, that makes karma seem a little selfish to me—like a person will only be kind and good to others to get to watch the feel-good reel at the end. But it can be so much more than the ending. If life is cyclical, so is kindness. Spin the wheel. And even if you land on 'bank-rupt,' try not to take it out on other humans... you never know who you will see again.

An overview of beliefs

TABLE OF INTERVIEWS

Perspective of:	Religion when young?
Lightworker	Catholic
Neurologist	Catholic
Hindu	Hinduism
Psychologist	Undisclosed
Humanist	Lutheran
Medical Mystery	Christian
Kundalini Yoga Musician	Catholic
Past Life Regressionist	None
Atheist	Methodist
Psychic Medium	Lutheran
P.I. Hypnotherapist	Catholic
Christian	Lutheran

Table A.1

TABLE OF INTERVIEWS (CONT'D)

PERSPECTIVE OF:	DO HUMANS HAVE A SOUL?
LIGHTWORKER	Yes
NEUROLOGIST	No
HINDU	Yes
PSYCHOLOGIST	Unsure
HUMANIST	No
MEDICAL MYSTERY	Yes
KUNDALINI YOGA MUSICIAN	Yes
PAST LIFE REGRESSIONIST	Yes
ATHEIST	No
PSYCHIC MEDIUM	Yes
P.I. HYPNOTHERAPIST	Yes
CHRISTIAN	Yes

Table A.2

TABLE OF INTERVIEWS (CONT'D)

PERSPECTIVE OF:	WHAT HAPPENS AFTER DEATH?
LIGHTWORKER	Light/energy "world," live again
NEUROLOGIST	Molecules disperse (physics)
HINDU	Spiritual realm, live again
PSYCHOLOGIST	Undisclosed
HUMANIST	Compost, but energy is not destroyed
MEDICAL MYSTERY	Heaven
KUNDALINI YOGA MUSICIAN	Ethereal place for souls, live again
PAST LIFE REGRESSIONIST	Energy realm, live again
ATHEIST	Dust
PSYCHIC MEDIUM	Spirit realm, live again
P.I. HYPNOTHERAPIST	The universe
CHRISTIAN	Heaven

Table A.3

TABLE OF INTERVIEWS (CONT'D)

PERSPECTIVE OF:	AFRAID OF DEATH?
LIGHTWORKER	No
NEUROLOGIST	No
HINDU	No
PSYCHOLOGIST	Unsure
HUMANIST	No
MEDICAL MYSTERY	No
KUNDALINI YOGA MUSICIAN	No
PAST LIFE REGRESSIONIST	No
ATHEIST	Yes & No
PSYCHIC MEDIUM	Yes & No
P.I. HYPNOTHERAPIST	No
CHRISTIAN	No

Table A.4

TABLE OF INTERVIEWS (CONT'D)

PERSPECTIVE OF:	BELIEVE IN REINCARNATION?
LIGHTWORKER	Yes
NEUROLOGIST	No
HINDU	Yes
PSYCHOLOGIST	Unsure
HUMANIST	No
MEDICAL MYSTERY	No
KUNDALINI YOGA MUSICIAN	Yes
PAST LIFE REGRESSIONIST	Yes
ATHEIST	No
PSYCHIC MEDIUM	Yes
P.I. HYPNOTHERAPIST	Unsure
CHRISTIAN	No

Table A.5

TABLE OF INTERVIEWS (CONT'D)

PERSPECTIVE OF:	BELIEVE IN SIGNS?
LIGHTWORKER	Yes
NEUROLOGIST	Perhaps a collective conscious
HINDU	Yes
PSYCHOLOGIST	No
HUMANIST	No
MEDICAL MYSTERY	Yes
KUNDALINI YOGA MUSICIAN	Yes
PAST LIFE REGRESSIONIST	Yes
ATHEIST	No
PSYCHIC MEDIUM	Yes
P.I. HYPNOTHERAPIST	Yes
CHRISTIAN	Yes

Table A.6

Overall Percentages from Table A

DO HUMANS HAVE A SOUL? Yes. 67%
AFRAID OF DEATH? No. 75%
BELIEVE IN REINCARNATION? No. 41%
BELIEVE IN SIGNS? Yes. 67%

Past Life Experiences in Detail

OCTOBER 10, 2016
FIRST EXPERIENCE
JEAN (MALE)
QUEBEC, CANADA

What are you wearing on your feet?

Boots. Big boots, trudging through the woods. I can hear them crunching things under my feet. I sense I have huge feet and I'm a huge man. My boots are brown with cleat-like bottoms.

Where are you going?

Back to the cabin.

Is anyone with you?

No, I'm alone. I'm always alone when I'm in the woods.

Where are you? What's around you?

Thick woods. Boulders. Pine trees and tall tree trunks surround the path. I see a single, spindly yellow flower blowing in the wind next to a boulder. (The yellow wildflower looks similar to a tiny daisy.) I sense that I'm on a mountain and there's a river below. But I'm pretty far up. Am I in America? Montana or Washington or Colorado maybe? I search for clues. I am white. I see the hairy backs of my callused hands. But I don't think I'm in America.

If you're in the countryside, what is the weather like?

(My body starts shivering.) It's cold. It's always cold. I don't know how that spindly little yellow flower is still alive with the frost every night. I think I'm wearing a warm hat. And I have my heavy flannel.

What do you look like?

I am huge. I am a lug of a man with black hair and a thick, black beard. Piercing blue eyes. Pretty expressionless. I don't smile much. But I'm not unhappy. I'm just stoic.

What are you wearing?

Black and red. Thick wool. I can see the checked pattern on my forearm. It's a fuzzy kind of wool.

What language do you speak?

I can't tell. I don't say much. I'm not a man of many words.

Are you carrying anything? Is anything in your hands?

Something slick and wooden is in my hands, slung over my right shoulder. The handle of an ax maybe?

What is your name?

Paul – no, I'm thinking of Paul Bunyan. John? No, I'm not John. I'm Jean. I'm French. Where in the world could I be a lumberjack type, tromping around the woods and speaking French? Canada! I'm French Canadian!

Do you have a spouse?

(I got really sad and remembered the love of my life was dead. But when I got to the cabin, I opened the door and she turned around from the fireplace pot, like she had done so many times before. I felt relief. She was still here. She wasn't gone yet.) I knew her all at once. I saw her smile at me and was flooded with so much knowledge about our love: She was a good cook. She was a wonderful wife. She kept me happy. She loved me endlessly. Adored me. Took care of everything for me so we could have a comfortable life. And I loved her more than I could say in words. I appreciated all that she did for me. She had wispy, strawberry-blonde hair and faint freckles. She always wiped her petite hands on her apron. She felt tiny in my arms, barely coming up to my armpit when we hugged. I would describe her as skinny—scrawny even. Frail and breakable, but she wasn't sick. Just dainty. Though she was scrappy and tough. Much like the wispy, yellow flower that fought through the frost. She was comfortable here in semi-isolation. Living in the cabin. I got the sense that I was her caretaker. Her protector. It was my job to keep her safe and fed, though she did all the cooking. She hummed when she cooked. I was probably condescending to her, but if she noticed—she didn't let me know. She was rarely cross with me. She had simple wants and they were all being met. She was my life and I was hers. I had the sense that we were very defined in our gender roles, but we liked it that way. We worked well together. We wanted to be together.

What is your spouse's name?

Mary... No, not Mary. Marie! Yes! This is my Marie. The love of my life. I brushed my huge knuckles down the hollow of her pale cheek and whispered something to her.

Do you have children?

Again, a smiling, happy feeling came over me. Yes. We have a daughter. One wonderful daughter who's light and frail and pale, just like her mother. She has freckles and wears her hair in braided pigtails. She always yells, "Papa!" when I come around the dirt path to the cabin and then throws her bony arms around my neck. She stuffs her face into my black beard. She adores me. And I adore her. She likes to jump off the wooden fence near the front window. I see her doing it now—lifting her skirts and hopping off with pigtails and skirt flapping. The huge sun is behind the house casting an afternoon glow around the whole homestead. It is so beautiful. So peaceful. My daughter chatters endlessly. *Papa this* and *Papa that*. I don't always listen. Marie and I are quiet. Our daughter is not.

About how old are you?

Marie and I are both in our thirties. Our daughter looked to be around eight.

What are your skills? What is your job or trade?

I see myself stringing up an animal carcass from the side of the cabin. I'm next to an enormous pile of logs that I cut myself with an ax. I see snowshoes. A sled full of pelts and furs.

Where do you live?

In our cabin with Marie and our daughter. I recall playing a stringed instrument near the fire, eating stew at a long wooden table, sleeping in the cot, with our daughter above in the loft.

What is one happy memory from this life?

Instantly, I was in the cabin at night. Marie and I were cuddled in front of the fire. We were having the most loving embrace I have ever known. I was whispering sweet nothings to her in French. About how happy I was. How in love I was. How happy I was that I was going to be a papa. How proud I was of her for creating life. How relieved that this was finally happening for us. She was gazing at me with such love I could feel it. (I actually started crying reliving this scene. A tear rolled down the side of my cheek.) Her head was resting on my upper arm and she had a small smile on her face. It was our own sacred, secret moment. Just us.

Alone in the cabin. The woods around us and our future ahead of us. Together, feeling absolutely complete and satisfied. Happy.

What is one sad memory from this life?

Instantly, I was standing outside the cabin, alone. I was old. I was waving at a vehicle (carriage? I don't recall horses. I only saw wheels in the dust.) My daughter was leaving home. She was going to do something great with her life—college? Boarding school? But I told her to leave me. I made her go and do more with her life now that Marie was gone. Marie had gone by then. I don't recall it being a bad death or even a surprising one. She was just gone and that was a fact. And when my daughter was leaving, she waved back to me—twisting around to see me as she drove away. And that was the last time I ever saw her. I didn't tell her I was ill. I knew she would come back to this cabin at some point and expect to find me, but I would already be gone. I thought I was protecting her this way.

How did this life end?

I flashed forward to not much farther in the future. I was back inside the cabin. It was a mess around me. Dirty and in decay. I was laying on the cot in the corner. I used to sleep up in the bunk, but I'd been too sick to climb the ladder. I was laying on a hard cot, covered in a white sheet pulled up to my chest. It was tight around me. Someone had tucked me in. I coughed into a wad of white rags. When the coughing fit had passed, I looked to see the rag covered in blood. This did not surprise me in the least. I was expecting that's what I'd see.

Are you alone when you die?

Yes. I wasn't supposed to be. Someone just said, "I'll be right back." But I knew they wouldn't be back in time. I knew the time was here. But I didn't feel afraid. I didn't feel bad to be alone. I was often alone. And it didn't matter anyway since I would soon find Marie again.

What are your last words?

I didn't say a thing.

Do you have any last thoughts as you die?

"I was a good man. I lived a good life. I am ready." And then I died. And I saw my light shoot straight up through the roof of the cabin and into the night's sky. Into the stars.

What happens to your body when you die?

I am put inside a wooden coffin. The plain, old kind like the ones in western movies.

Is anyone attending your funeral?

Yes. Neighbors and acquaintances dressed in black. No one special. My daughter doesn't know I'm gone yet. Marie is already gone.

Now picture the world beyond death. Are you there?

I am! Everything is so white it's actually light. There are slight shadows all around me and I don't hear or see anyone, but I know they are all my loves from all my lives. All around me. Enveloping me in a pure love.

How did you get there?

My light shot up from my body—from my chest, I think. All the way up, I was focused on Marie. "I'm coming, Marie! I'm coming!" As soon as I break through from the starry, outerspace-like night into the light, another orb of light is sucked toward me like a magnet. I know it to be Marie! We whirl around in a circle so quickly that we make yin yang with our lights. And then we burst into a kind of fireworks of pure, white lights—drifting back down and becoming our own selves again; each a separate orb of light. Immediately released from all the pain, worry, loneliness, longing, emotion. And then I feel nothing. I think nothing. There is peace or calm, but not really because those things have no meaning in the abstract light.

What can the you today learn from your past life? Why are you seeing it today?

My brain searches, but I'm not sure. Maybe I smother my children with love because I know true loss of love from the past? Did we have several miscarriages or stillborns? Our daughter was sacred when she was a baby. We were both old when we had her. But I don't feel sure that's my message.

Are there any symbols you need to see today?

I only saw the pattern of my black and red flannel.

Are there any words you need to hear today?

Instantly, I was back in the cabin. (This scene was more like watching a movie than living it.) I was taking a huge rifle from hooks near the loft bunk's ladder. Marie and my daughter were in their nightgowns, huddled together on our bed in the corner. Terrified. It was night and I heard a pack of wolves howling outside. I knew they were gray wolves. And then as if a character on TV suddenly turned and addressed you by name, Jean looked directly into me/ at me—eyes to eyes somehow, very intimately—and loudly pumped his rifle (the sound echoed in the cabin CH-CH), "DON'T BE AFRAID!" he ordered in English with a heavy French accent. (The only time he/I spoke English.) His blue eyes were swirling with emotion. I felt like I was him again. And I was terrified too, but I knew I was the one who had to protect my family. I was going out into the woods at night to scare off wolves. Because I had to. And I knew I could do it.

NOVEMBER 16, 2016
SECOND EXPERIENCE
VINNY (MALE)
BROOKLYN, NY

What are you wearing on your feet?

Work boots. Dusty, crusty brown ones.

Where are you going?

Back up to the top of the site. (I see the skeleton of a sky-scraper. I'm heading up to the top to work.)

Is anyone with you?

All my boys are around me. I'm one of many workers at the site...iron workers? Welders?

Where are you? What's around you?

Maybe New York as it's coming into existence? We all have heavy Italian accents and black hair. We are very close. Like family. Maybe some are my family.

If you're in the city, what is the weather like?

Chilly. A little drizzly. But nothin' that would stop us from working a long day.

What do you look like?

Thin, but with thick arms. I think I box as a hobby. I see my arms as a thing of pride. I show them off every chance I get.

What are you wearing?

Overalls, white T-shirt and work boots. Maybe a hat?

What language do you speak?

English, but I think I also know Italian.

Are you carrying anything? Is anything in your hands?

My hands are always calloused with scabby knuckles. Some-times I'm carrying tools or equipment or a metal lunchbox.

What is your name?

Vinny...Vincent...Vincenzo.

Do you have a spouse?

Nah. Dames are lame.

What is your spouse's name?

Don't have one.

Do you have children?

Nah.

About how old are you?

In my twenties. My prime. I feel healthy and fit and great!

What are your skills? What is your job or trade?

I build skyscrapers. I have great pride for my trade. I love what I do and the attention it gains me. Me and the boys eat lunch on top of the world! I feel chest-bursting pride about building something that will be a part of New York forever. I love America.

Where do you live?

Brooklyn. But I work in New York City. I live alone in an empty, small room in an apartment building that's filled with other Italian immigrants. Just a cot for a bed and a small table with a lamp—that's all that's in my place.

What is one happy memory from this life?

I hone in on a small, hot, crowded bar. Me and a group of other iron workers are drinking, laughing and telling off stories. I'm in Daube's Bar night after night after working on some skyscraper. But this was the night that all eyes were on me. I knew I had just finished boxing in the alley to make a quick buck. I took the louse's money and spent it on my boys. My bloody lip didn't stop me from putting one foot up on the table and holding my beer over the round table of guys to retell the play by play. I knew I had a real boxing match coming up with Johnny Blue. The guys ribbed me that I didn't stand a chance, but I was macho and cocky and felt no hesitation that I was going to beat him.

And have a chance to be a real boxer. All eyes were on me while I cracked jokes about curvy blondes and jabbed the other guys' wives. Everyone laughed and ate up everything I had to say.

What is one sad memory from this life?

I couldn't hone in on anything specific.

How did this life end?

I was on a high floor of a skyscraper, inside. The building was half-done. I could feel a strong wind blowing in from the side with no walls. It was the day we were mixing and pouring concrete. It came in huge, heavy sacks. One of the guys called for me to start carrying them over. We'd just used a pully up an empty elevator shaft to get them up this far. I'd disassembled the pulley and tossed it aside. I did take a long look down the empty shaft. Then, I decided I had taken too long and the guys were all waiting. So instead of grabbing just one sack of concrete powder, I put my hands under two sacks and hoisted. I knew my arms could handle it. But I didn't realize how close to the open shaft I was standing. The weight and thrust of the two sacks being slung over my shoulder made me tip backwards just enough that I lost my balance. I dropped the sacks and tried to catch myself, but I was already falling backwards down the shaft. I knew I was about to die. But it felt like a slow fall. I heard the sound—horrible, horrible sound—of my body landing at the bottom on the concrete.

Are you alone when you die?

Yep.

What are your last words?

Don't think I said anything.

Do you have any last thoughts as you die?

I was angry I wouldn't get to box Johnny Blue and angry I

was dying so young. Angry I didn't get to do so many things I wanted to do.

What happens to your body when you die?

I'm not sure. I was too pissed off to try to see.

Is anyone attending your funeral?

Don't know.

Now picture the world beyond death. Are you there?

Not really. I'm still stewing about how stupid my life and death were.

What can the you today learn from your past life? Why are you seeing it today?

Vinny was leaning in the skyscraper near the open elevator shaft. He turned and looked at me with a disgusted and annoyed look and said, "Well, this was a wasted life."

MARCH 1, 2018
THIRD EXPERIENCE
SWEET BEA (FEMALE)
MEMPHIS, TN

What are you wearing on your feet?

Black...nurses shoes? Like from the 1960s. Shoes worn and bowed due to being walked on by someone over-weight...and with bunions. I saw I was a large, black woman in a dress and stockings.

Where are you going?

I'm hustling down a city street in the summer. Heading to the laundromat. My purse keeps slipping down my shoulder. I'm sweaty. I'm in a particular hurry because I want to get there in time to see the gleaming silver bus arrive in town.

Is anyone with you?

Not at the moment. I'll see Lottie-dah in a bit.

Where are you? What's around you?

Memphis, Tennessee! (I declare in a proud and loud Southern accent.) I get to the laundromat and am greeted by the other housekeepers. We're all plenty thrilled about the person on the bus arriving in town. When we see the silver bus come streaking down the street, we all rush to the window to catch a peak. There's excitement in the air. We all know we are witnessing history. After the bus passes, we all joke and chat while we do the laundry, fanning ourselves and laughing.

If you're in the city, what is the weather like?

I already told ya it was HOT.

What do you look like?

Aiyee...not as good as I used to. But plenty nice. Don't you worry 'bout that none. (Sweet Bea constantly made my conscious brain laugh and smile. If someone had been watching my reactions, I would have looked ridiculous. I was really enjoying this experience!)

What are you wearing?

I looked down to see a plain cotton type of dress spattered with tiny blue flowers. I had an apron on, slightly sagging stockings and a slip under my dress. I also had a hat with a flower.

What language do you speak?

English! But the good kind. The SOUTHERN kind.

Are you carrying anything? Is anything in your hands?

I've still got this darn purse'a mine that never stays put. I also have the laundry bags for the missus.

What is your name?

SWEET Bea! ...Beatrice Palmer (Pahl-ma).

Do you have a spouse?

Yes, I do. Don't know that I'll keep him.

What is your spouse's name?

Jerry.

Do you have children?

Oh, yes! Light of my life! (Sweet Bea smiled so big and clasped hands together, excited to talk about her babies.) My beautiful, intelligent Lottie. Well, we call her Lottie-dah on account she's gonna be so *well to do*. She's goin' to Junior College soon. And I have a son, too. Jerry, Jr. He's in jail for bein' stupid though. He takes after his father.

About how old are you?

In my fifties.

What are your skills? What is your job or trade?

I'm the house manager for the missus. I caretake, cook, clean and do the chore work. I'm also a leader in our beautiful Baptist church. I keep mighty busy.

Where do you live?

Round back of the missus. Mostly I just sleep there though.

What is one happy memory from this life?

I was in my church, surrounded by the community and congregation. It was packed and hot. We were all dressed up in our best clothes. At the front of the church was a handsome young man, nervous and waiting for my Lottie-girl. She was about to walk down the aisle. When I turned to look, I saw I was with a new man. It was not Jerry, but my new beau. He was beaming with pride along with me as Lottie walked down the aisle of our expansive, stain-glassed church. It was a very large church. One of the biggest in Memphis. And it was ours. And I couldn't have been more proud or excited if it was my own wedding.

What is one sad memory from this life?

I saw snips of moments in my life when I was being harassed and hassled. Snips of racist comments spit at me through open windows of passing cars. Flashes of Lottie crying cuz of what people said to her. It all made me so mad that I began to do something about it. I got involved in civil rights groups. I felt sure we could make it right. The bad parts made me a fighter because I wanted everyone to understand that all people should be treated as humans.

How did this life end?

I was humming in the missus's kitchen. Dropping cookie batter on a pan, making a whole lot of drop cookies for the big to-do at church. I had the door open to get some breeze to blow into the hot kitchen. I wiped my hands on my apron and picked up the pan. As I turned to slip the pan into the oven, I had a stabbing pain in my chest. I dropped the pan and it ricocheted off the edge of the counter in a thunderous crash, sending balls of dough raining down around me. I was clutching a wad of my dress at my chest as I slid to the ground, gasping for air. And then I was just gone from the scene.

Are you alone when you die?

Yes, though there are others in the house and around, no one was with me when I died.

What are your last words?

Sweet Jesus!

Do you have any last thoughts as you die?

Lord, let my family do right. Let them have more good times than bad. I did my best here. Please take care of them.

What happens to your body when you die?

I'm placed in a fancy coffin, much more than I needed. My

family prepares a large funeral for me. They serve pie afterwards.

Is anyone attending your funeral?

Oh, yes. A whole of Memphis is there! All my family, my congregation, my civil rights troop, the ladies from the laundromat...everyone. I feel very loved.

Now picture the world beyond death. Are you there?

I am. It is a light world of sorts. I notice I no longer have an accent. Or feelings. Or really, thoughts. I'm hovering in a vast field of orbs.

How did you get there?

I shot straight up from Sweet Bea's body, perhaps from her stomach area?

What can the you today learn from your past life? Why are you seeing it today?

We gotta do more. We have the ability to do more.

Are there any symbols you need to see today?

I see Sweet Bea standing in church, holding a hymnal and singing her heart out to the Lord, believing without a doubt there was something out there to praise.

Are there any words you need to hear today?

Sweet Bea was back in the laundromat, humming. She stopped folding clothes to look at me. "I got closer, child. I did right by us. I did alllll-right." She nodded with a smile and went back to humming and folding.

OCTOBER 5, 2018
FOURTH EXPERIENCE
GREGORY (MALE)
LIVERPOOL, ENGLAND

What are you wearing on your feet?

My feet were in shiny (or just wet?) black shoes. Looking up from there, I saw pressed gray trousers and a "Sherlock Holmes" cape.

Where are you going?

Off to see the widow. (I say in a heavy English accent.)

I was walking down a bustling street filled with horses and black carriages, vendors, children and tightly-fitted houses, though I knew they were not houses. Tenements?

Is anyone with you?

Not at the moment.

Where are you? What's around you?

Liverpool. I'm walking through the streets. I looked up to see the docks ahead of me. The road goes straight out to the water, where they dock the ships.

When I got to where I was going, I knocked with my cane. I was ushered in by a tired-looking lady in many layers of skirt. She wouldn't look me in the face at all. We sat on her Victorian sofa together while many children ran in and out, yelling and rushing up and down the stairs around us. I knew she was a widow. I knew I was holding flowers for her. I placed my hand on top of her hand, relishing the feel of another human in my very lonely life.

She didn't look my way, not once. She was upset with me. I was trying to understand the scene. Were we together? Was she my wife? Were these my children? But the answer to all was no.

If you're in the city, what is the weather like?

Cold, windy and always dreary.

What do you look like?

I had a ring of hair around my head, bald at the top, with a bushy mustache and decaying, yellow teeth. I was terribly pale. I often wore a shiny top hat.

What are you wearing?

Why, I already told you.

What language do you speak?

English, of course.

Are you carrying anything? Is anything in your hands?

I had a black cane with a golden tip that hit the cobblestone with every step. The top of the cane was shaped like a diamond, that fit perfectly in my hand. In my other hand, I held a small bouquet of vibrant, baby blue flowers. They were the only bit of color in the gray, hazy, drizzly scene. They were for the widow.

What is your name?

Gregory Smythe. (He spoke in a formal, introductory tone. I think he bowed.)

Do you have a spouse?

My wife was a blonde named Patricia (Pah-Tree-see-ah). She died when very young. I didn't seem to spend much time thinking about her or how she died or feel any sort of regret, sorrow or sadness. She was just not in my life for many, many years at this point. I knew I was courting the widow, but didn't have strong feelings about her. I was just relieved to have a woman be interested in me.

Do you have children?

No. No heirs.

About how old are you?

"Fo'tee foe (44)," he stated in his accent. (The first time I got an exact age.)

What are your skills? What is your job or trade?

I am proud of my business smarts. I am a successful banker.

Where do you live?

Liverpool, near the docks.

Were there any major events that occurred in your lifetime?

I saw a crew building a supremely high clock tower on or for a building. They were using wood and I shook my head at the thought of it all coming down in a fire.

What is one happy memory from this life?

I was suddenly standing on the deck of a ship at those very docks I'd walked past every day of my life in Liverpool. I was waving goodbye, I think even using a handkerchief to wave, but quickly stopped waving because I felt stupid waving to no one. No one was there to see me off. No one cared where I went. I had said goodbye to the widow and, beyond her, I had no one.

I remember being filled to the brim with excitement and anticipation and the lust for true adventure. I looked out to where the sea met the sky. (I said that a lot to myself. I'm off to discover where the sea meets the sky.) When I did, I saw the letter "G." I was going somewhere very foreign, perhaps with a jungle, to explore. My conscious mind offered suggestion—Greenland? No. Galapagos? No. Ghana? Maybe, where's that?

What is one sad memory from this life?

I moved forward to see myself sitting in my little cabin on the ship. It was tiny with just a cot, a built-in table and screwed in chair looking at a porthole. There was some sort of time piece that I had affixed to the table to keep track of time. I had been on the ship for weeks, maybe months. I had gotten sea sick many times. Out the porthole, where the sea met the sky, the scene rocked and went askew. I was writing with an ink pen... there was an ink well in the desk maybe? I thought I was writing a letter, but Gregory quickly butted in, "Now who in the devil would I be writing to?" I was keeping a log; a journal of the journey. I was getting close to arriving. It would be treacherous, dangerous. I was meeting other affluent white men there. Some sort of safari came to mind, but I don't think that was it. I didn't feel like I was a hunter. Some sort of exploration or maybe mapmaking or recording of uncharted territory felt more accurate.

How did this life end?

I was in a white canvass tent held up by rough beams of wood, lying in a wooden, sagging cot with a white sheet over me. I was only wearing one-piece, white underwear that were a tank top and shorts. My mustache was mostly white now. I was so thin and somehow paler. I was sweating and sweating. The hottest I had ever been. I wanted the sheet off, but the nurse had it on to keep many of the bugs off of us. Yes, us. There were several of us white men in the cots in the tent. We were all cared for by one young, black-haired nurse. She was our angel. When she placed her hand on my bare arm, I realized it was the first skin-to-skin contact I had experienced in years! And I was dying, that I was sure of. We were all dying of an infectious disease. I was so worried the kind nurse would get it from us. I somehow knew it was yellow fever, but no one was calling it that.

Are you alone when you die?

I'm unsure. I was in and out of consciousness and I don't recall the exact moment I left my body.

What are your last words?

I said nothing.

Do you have any last thoughts as you die?

Rambling thoughts of regret and negativity toward my choices.

What happens to your body when you die?

(In my meditative state, I got very choked up. In real life, my breathing quickened and my face scrunched up. It felt painful to review this portion.) I watched as they wrapped us dead old chaps up in the white sheets, threw us in a pile between the tent and the jungle and burned us all. They had to be sure we wouldn't infect others. But I was just burned and forgotten. No one knew I was dead. No one even knew where I was. But no one cared I was dead. It was such an empty, empty life. I wondered who would get my money? I had expected to return. I hadn't set anything up before my departure.

Is anyone attending your funeral?

Alas, there was no funeral.

Now picture the world beyond death. Are you there?

Yes, it is the same glowing energy world as I've experienced before.

How did you get there?

I'm uncertain, but I feel like I meandered up with the smoke of my burning body...

What can the you today learn from your past life? Why are you seeing it today?

I saw Gregory standing on the ship's deck, watching the horizon creep closer. He stopped smiling at the wind and adventure and turned to ME. In his heavy English accent, he said, "Freedom is NOT mo' impo'tant than love."

And I somehow knew he was using the term "freedom"

to mean having financial freedom and no one to obligate you. He knew it seemed thrilling—being able to sail off into the horizon because you wanted to and because you could. It was amazing! But what was it without someone to share life with? Not even in a romantic-love way, but in general. No connections with anyone. No children, friends, mates. What an empty place.

Are there any words you need to hear today?

Gregory shook his head over and over muttering, "I'm sorry I wasted another life. I'm sorry. Don't waste another life, love. Don't waste another one."

Acknowledgments

I N A BOOK that spends so much time talking about experiences and gratitude, the acknowledgements cannot be overstated.

In alphabetical order, thank you to my open and authentic interviewees Aileen Abliss, Cecilia Baldwin, Richard Benack, Britt Brill, Eric Christopher, Melissa Divine, Bassem Fadlia, Brigitte Holzinger, Kitty Karn, Audrey Kingstrom, Jon Maki, Pooja Mamgain, Brinn McManus, Liborio Parrino and Stephanie Zvan. Without your wisdom, this book would not be.

Special thanks to the love of my life, Craig, for being such a tremendous supporter and all-around good sport, as well as my madcap children for adding so much to my perspective.

I also thank my parents, Paul and Mary, for instilling a curiosity and allowing the freedom to be the "weird kid" so I could and would pursue my strange interests.

My team of readers, proofreaders, editors and supporters also deserves a huge thank you: Vicki Snyder, Brent Hilgart and Rebecca Hoffman. Thank you to LaVonne, Sondra, Tracy and Nicole for giving me and my project valuable time and perspectives.

Kathleen May, thank you for being a tremendous editor, truth-teller and troubleshooter.

Additional thanks must go to my cover designer, germancreative, and to Phillip Gessert, for the beautiful book interior. Thank you for formatting my words into a lovely book.

I'd like to offer a special thank you to those who have passed away, yet were still a part of this journey—Uncle Jim, Steven, Brynn and those unnamed—thank you for allowing me to tell some of your story.

My final words of gratitude go to all the wise humans quoted and referred to within this book. It's only as we collaborate that we can discover the full beauty and knowledge our collective has to offer. Here's to humans! We're pretty great.

Index

About the Author

GINA DEWINK IS the author of *Time in My Pocket*, a time travel fiction novel. *Human, with a Side of Soul* is her first nonfiction book. She is a contributing writer for several mediums, including *Thrive Global*, *Rochester Women Magazine* and *507 Magazine*. She also tells the stories of nonprofits, as she's worked in nonprofit communications since 2001, including a radio documentary aired early in her career. She lives in Minnesota with her husband and two young children. You can learn more at ginadewink.com or by following Gina on Twitter (@ginadewink) and Facebook (ginadewinkauthor).

REVIEWS ARE PRICELESS

IF YOU ENJOYED *Human, with a Side of Soul: One Woman's Soul Quest through Open-Minded Interviews*, please consider leaving a review on Amazon or other retailer websites.

Learn more at ginadewink.com or follow Gina on Twitter and Facebook.

Human, with a Side of Soul is also available in ebook.

Discussion questions

1. Which perspective did you most agree with? In your opinion, which seemed the most farfetched?
2. What new concepts did you learn about? Any you will continue to study?
3. How would you have acted differently if you had conducted the soul interviews?
4. What do you think the author's purpose was in writing this book? What ideas was she trying to get across?
5. Which person in the book would you most like to meet? Why?
6. What aspects of the journey could you most relate to?
7. What feelings did this book evoke for you?
8. Were there parts of the book you thought were unique, out of place, thought-provoking or disturbing?
9. If you got the chance to ask the author of this book one question, what would it be?
10. What was the major takeaway the book left you with? Would you share it?